The Best
Men's Stage Monologues
# of 2001

Smith and Kraus *Books for Actors*

MONOLOGUE AUDITION SERIES

The Best Men's / Women's Stage Monologues of 2000
The Best Men's / Women's Stage Monologues of 1999
The Best Men's / Women's Stage Monologues of 1998
The Best Men's / Women's Stage Monologues of 1997
The Best Men's / Women's Stage Monologues of 1996
The Best Men's / Women's Stage Monologues of 1995
The Best Men's / Women's Stage Monologues of 1994
The Best Men's / Women's Stage Monologues of 1993
The Best Men's / Women's Stage Monologues of 1992
The Best Men's / Women's Stage Monologues of 1991
The Best Men's / Women's Stage Monologues of 1990
One Hundred Men's / Women's Stage Monologues from the 1980s
2 Minutes and Under: Character Monologues for Actors Volumes I and II
Monologues from Contemporary Literature: Volume I
Monologues from Classic Plays 468 BC to 1960 AD
100 Great Monologues from the Renaissance Theatre
100 Great Monologues from the Neo-Classical Theatre
100 Great Monologues from the 19th Century Romantic and Realistic Theatres
The Ultimate Audition Series Volume I: 222 Monologues, 2 Minutes & Under
The Ultimate Audition Series Volume II: 222 Monologues, 2 Minutes & Under
    from Literature

YOUNG ACTOR MONOLOGUE SERIES

Cool Characters for Kids: 71 One-Minute Monologues
Great Scenes and Monologues for Children, Volumes I and II
Great Monologues for Young Actors, Volumes I and II
Short Scenes and Monologues for Middle School Actors
Multicultural Monologues for Young Actors
The Ultimate Audition Series for Middle School Actors Vol.I: 111 One-Minute
    Monologues
The Ultimate Audition Series for Teens Vol. I: 111 One-Minute Monologues
The Ultimate Audition Series for Teens Vol.II: 111 One-Minute Monologues
The Ultimate Audition Series for Teens Vol.III: 111 One-Minute Monologues
The Ultimate Audition Series for Teens Vol.IV: 111 One-Minute Monologues
The Ultimate Audition Series for Teens Vol.V: 111 One-Minute Monologues
    from Shakespeare
Wild and Wacky Characters for Kids: 60 One-Minute Monologues

If you require prepublication information about upcoming Smith and Kraus books, you may receive our semiannual catalogue, free of charge, by sending your name and address to *Smith and Kraus Catalogue, PO Box 127, Lyme, NH 03768. Or call us at (800) 895-4331; fax (603) 643-6431.*

The Best
Men's Stage Monologues
of 2001

edited by D. L. Lepidus

MONOLOGUE AUDITION SERIES

A SMITH AND KRAUS BOOK

Published by Smith and Kraus, Inc.
177 Lyme Road, Hanover, NH 03755
www.SmithKraus.com

First Edition: July 2003
10 9 8 7 6 5 4 3 2 1

Cover illustration by Lisa Goldfinger
Cover design by Julia Hill Gignoux

The Monologue Audition Series
ISSN 1067-134X
ISBN 1-57525-351-8

**NOTE: These scenes are intended to be used for audition and class study;
permission is not required to use the material for those purposes. However,
if there is a paid performance of any of the scenes included in this book,
please refer to the permissions acknowledgment pages 81–85 to locate the
source that can grant permission for public performance.**

Contents

Foreword

If you have purchased this book, or if you are thinking of purchasing this book, you are probably an acting student, a teacher of acting students, a professional actor, or working to become a professional actor. You are looking for material to work on in class or to use for auditions. Hopefully, you have found Smith and Kraus's monologue anthologies suited to your needs in the past. It is my hope, as the new editor of this series, that you will find this book even *more* useful.

Almost all of the monologues in this book are from readily available published plays; so now, you will be able to read the whole play as you work on your role. In the case of material not from published plays, we have tried to include contact information for the author — or we will gladly refer any inquiry about getting the whole script directly to him or her.

Almost all the monologues in this book are about characters close to the actual age of the actors who will use this book — making the material easier for them to understand and use.

In closing, I would like to offer my profuse gratitude to Marisa Smith and Eric Kraus for entrusting me with the daunting but hugely rewarding task of editing this book. I would like to thank Elizabeth Monteleone for her kind assistance in procuring permissions to use the material herein. And I offer thanks, most especially, to all the playwrights and agents who graciously gave their permission to print these scenes from their wonderful plays.

— D. L. Lepidus

The Altruists
Nicky Silver

Comic

Ethan (twenties to thirties)

Ethan is telling off his friend Sydney, a woman of about the same age.

ETHAN: Sydney, it's your life. Fine. Do what you want. Stay in bed all
day. If that's how you want to live your life, I can't stop you! But it
would do you some good, it would do you a world of good to get
out of that bed, out of this house. It would do you a lot of good to
see yourself as part of something bigger, better, something more important than you. You, you, you, you, you! Not everything is about
you. The earth's pull doesn't emanate from you, nor does the change
of seasons, nor the ebb of tides. You're one person, Sydney! A crumb,
a speck, a molecule, a *mark* on a molecule that means nothing. But
do you ever put yourself out for the greater good? No. When I asked
you to come to protest police brutality, did you? No, you turned up
your nose. You snubbed the homeless and cancer research and AIDS
funding and immigration, and the taxi drivers and free needles and
the dolphins and animal testing and school funding and day-care cen-
ters and American Indians and gay rights, and black rights and
women's rights and Spanish rights and Swedish rights and Chinese
rights and handicapped rights and Armenia and Bosnia and arms for
hostages and Mothers Against Drunk Driving. You snubbed welfare
cutbacks and arts cutbacks and housing cutbacks and school cutbacks
and . . . Medicare and Medicaid and needle exchange and govern-
ment free cheese! And when Gustavo needed a bone marrow trans-
plant, were you interested? You were not. Because it wasn't about you.
You chose instead to lie there. That's right, lie there. Inert. Wallow-
ing in the juices of your bourgeois squalor. Lie there like a corpse,
like a beached sea creature, like a walrus — like the walruses you re-
fused to help by protesting their poaching and slaughter for ivory
tusks. What's wrong with you, Sydney? What is wrong with you?

Anton in Show Business
Jane Martin

Comic

Don Blount (any age over thirty-five)

> *This play was written to be performed by an all-female cast, playing both men and women. As this character is male, I have included it in the men's monologue book. Don could be any age over, say, thirty-five. He is a tobacco company executive in charge of charitable arts donations.*

DON: Don Blount of Albert & Sons Tobacco calling for Martha Graham. Then why is it called the Martha Graham Dance Company? Oh. No, I knew that. Little joke. Listen, the grant's in the mail. Yes. Well, it's our pleasure to support a dance company of your caliber and if you might find an opportunity to mention to the chairman of your board that we'd be thrilled if she'd tell her brother the congressman to stop sodomizing the tobacco industry just because he's personally in the pocket of the HMO's, I think you'd find your grant is definitely renewable. My pleasure. *(Don hangs up the phone, picks it back up, and dials.)* Mom, it's Don. Your son Don. I need the favor, Mom. I know we did it yesterday, but I'm feeling a little alienated . . . a little remote. Wonderful. Good. I knew I could count on you. Momma. Ready? All right, light it up, Mom. Inhale, Mom. Would I encourage you to smoke if there was any danger? That's right, I wouldn't. I would never harm my mom. I must be a good person if I would never harm my mom. If I'm a good person, it must be all right to do what I do. Thanks, I feel a lot better. Put it out now, Momma. Everything's all right. I feel damn good. Go back on the oxygen, Ma. See you Sunday.

Anton in Show Business

Jane Martin

Comic

Joe Bob (forties to fifties)

> *This play was written to be performed by an all-female cast, playing both men and women. As this character is male, I have included it in this book. Joe Bob is a white southerner, probably forties to fifties but could be younger. He is the chairman of the board of directors of a small professional theater company and he's had it with their artsy-fartsy pretensions.*

JOE BOB: Damn woman! You got no more sense than a hog on ice! I been pourin' my money an' the money of my friends down your double-talk rathole since Jesus was a pup, so my wife could drag me down here to see plays nobody can understand with a buncha people I would never invite to dinner, on the basis it creates some quality of life I'm supposed to have since I figgered out how to make some money. Half the time, that stuff doesn't have a story, and it's been five years since you done one takes place in a kitchen, which is the kind all of us like. The rest of the time it's about how rich people is bad and Democrats is good and white people is stupid and homosexuals have more fun an' we should get rid of the corporations an' eat grass an' then, by God, you wonder why you don't have a big audience! Now you just blew 15 percent of your budget 'cause you riled up the tobacco interest, plus you got the colored rattlin' on my cage, and as of this precise minute, you are out of luck, out of work an' outta San Antonio, Texas. See, I am closin' us down, lockin' the door, an' then, by God, we can go back to hittin' each other up to give to the United Way where it will, by God, do some poor handicap some actual, measurable good, an' I won't have to hear anybody say "aesthetic" from one year to the goddamned next! Now, vaya con Dios, darlin'.

Bafo
Tom Strelich

Dramatic

P.K. (thirties to fifties)

> *This is a wild farce about a hostage situation involving a disgruntled ex-employee of a company. P.K. is that employee. He is holding some of his former coworkers hostage.*

P.K.: Where's the threat? Is history wasted on you? Haven't you learned anything? You haven't got a prayer. Unless you have a threat. Don't you remember? Why did our knuckle-dragging forefathers pick up that first blunt instrument? Why did they paint their faces and put antlers on their heads and do the hokey pokey around the campfire? *(No response.)* Because they were afraid of something: lightning, thunder, saber-toothed tiger. They had a threat. A real, credible, undeniable threat. So they had a need. Before Jesus, before Mohammed, before Jehovah, before the pagan gods, demigods, animal gods, before all the great protectors, you had one, single unifying force in the space-time continuum . . . And you *know* what it is? Don't you? That's right, the boogey man. We didn't start praying out of joy or gratitude, but because we were scared shitless. All of mankind's accomplishments, religion, art, civilization. *(Pointing at a commemorative photo.)* I-C-B-M's that go bump in the night — all sprout from the same cowering seed. When the archangels appeared before the shepherds in a blinding light a hundred generations ago and told them that Jesus Christ, the Son of man, the blessed redeemer, was being born that very night, did they rise up and weep for joy at the gift to mankind of salvation and eternal life? Heck no. They shrank back in fright and fell on their bellies in supplication and submission, and begged for mercy. People back then knew what to do when in the presence of a terrifying, but possibly benevolent, entity. What would people do nowadays if an avenging angel or a burning bush, say, appeared before them? Probably nothing. Probably just say, "wow" and wait for Connie Toyota and News Team Eleven to show up. Nothing makes us fall on our bellies anymore. Only one of those goddamn things *(The AK-47.)* . . . not that I'm suggesting. But you would if I asked, right?

This is my point. Threat comes before everything. Because life itself is a threat — its very existence threatens its loss. Do you see the cosmic unity of that, the indivisible duality? This has been such an illuminating day for me, everybody should do this. *(Beat.)* You haven't got a PRAYER if you haven't got FAITH. And you can't have FAITH . . . *(Shaking his gun.)* unless you have a THREAT!

The Bohemian Seacoast
Don Nigro

Comic

The Corpse (fifties)

> *This is a wild comedy about a scholar intent on solving the "Shakespeare mystery." The speaker is the corpse of William Shakespeare.*

THE CORPSE: Victory? Victory? And just what pathetic victory do you expect to snatch from me? Do you believe you're the only one who's spent their life being patronized by pompous dunderheads? Do you really know what it is to be a playwright? Do you know how many jackals and hyenas await you at every turn, ready to steal from you, plagiarize you, and blather shit-encrusted moronic fashionable theories at you? Do you know what it is to have every semiliterate cabbage head in the universe forever telling you what to write and how to write it and why you must change what you've written and how they know better than you what your play should be and shouldn't be, gibbering snot-brained clabberheads who can themselves barely scrawl their own names, who call you arrogant for objecting to the ritual dismemberment of your life's work written in blood to satisfy their own gargantuan fatuous flatulent vomit-sucking egos? Christ, woman, I spent my life in the theater. I've got more knives sticking in my back than Julius Caesar. And now some stupid, stupid woman from Akron wants to desecrate my tomb to find some damned imaginary coded message from Queen Elizabeth or Pliny the Elder or some wretched person placed there especially for her personal gratification to prove some crackbrained theory about Francis Bacon and Henry the Eighth concocting my plays on a Sunday afternoon with Sir Walter Raleigh and Attilla the Hun after a spirited tennis match, and just for fun inserting complex and cryptic cyphers in them proving that I was in fact Cleopatra's Egyptian uncle's great grandson, the heir to the Welsh throne? What is the matter with you people? Must you continue to suck out my blood even after I am mercifully dead? Do you not see that your obsession is but vile and pathetic snobbery and ignorance and secret self-loathing and hatred of creation itself and all who give their lives to it? It is the monumental jealousy and cowardice of such people which devours me like maggots. It is creation that is beauty and is joy, in the midst of all the muckheap of one's life. You have wedded yourself to futility and destruction, and your kingdom is a tomb much darker and more dismal than mine can ever be. For Christ's sake, woman, get yourself a life.

The Butterfly Collection
Theresa Rebeck

Dramatic

Paul (about sixty)

> *Paul is a famous novelist with a terrible case of writer's block. He was played in the original Off Broadway production by Brian Murray. He is talking to his son, Ethan, who is a semisuccessful professional actor.*

PAUL: I had nothing to do with you? Do you even hear yourself? Go do your play, the theater deserves you. But don't kid yourself into thinking you're your own man. You might have been, if there were more to you. But you're just what I made you. Feels good doesn't it, going off to do your *art,* you're in the heat of it, I am too, it's all going better and the rest of it is suddenly gone. The self-loathing. The contempt, hating yourself so much that the rest of humanity has to bear the brunt of it, the fear of death or even worse, *failure,* worse than that even *mediocrity,* hovering out there. For half a moment, perhaps, it occurs to you to snap out of it, but change is a fleet thought, isn't it, fuck the chance to find something in yourself, so that when you die you're not just looking at the end with terror in your bones, trying to figure out why all of it, fame, awards, the luck even just to do it, every day, why that just didn't add up to *more.* Why the sheer beauty of just being alive never lifted your heart beyond — this.

The Butterfly Collection
Theresa Rebeck

Dramatic

Ethan (forty)

Ethan, a professional actor, is on the phone with his agent.

ETHAN: Absolutely not. No. I told you two weeks ago, two weeks ago, Sam — I am not sabotaging anything! If they want to offer me the part, I will happily accept it, it's a wonderful part even for three hundred fucking dollars a week — No, I'm not going to meet with him, that's ridiculous, either he wants me to do the part, or he doesn't, having a cup of coffee with the man isn't going to convince him that I can act! All he can learn from a meeting is whether or not I look like my headshot, and I'm not driving three hours into the city for that. Yes, it is, three solid hours; they're doing construction on the Cross Bronx. Yes, they are! What am I — I am relaxing, Sam. That is what I am doing here. I am relaxing in the country with my family. Look, it's my brothers' birthday and my mother is making a big thing of it, and she disapproves of people who do business on the phone after six, so I've got to go. Yes, I will but I'm not going to change my mind. Seriously, I find it ridiculous that the instant I insist on being treated with the barest pretence of respect, everyone acts like I'm crazy. It's a very sick business we're in. Good-bye.

The Butterfly Collection
Theresa Rebeck

Dramatic

Ethan (forty)

> *Ethan, a professional actor, is on the phone with his agent.*

ETHAN: No, absolutely not. He's seen my work — well, then fuck him
if he hasn't seen me in something over the last six years, where the
hell has he been, running around the regionals? Oh, *London.* Of
course, *London,* that's so much more impressive, he's probably been
over their directing *Joseph and the Amazing Technicolor Dreamcoat,*
and he thinks that makes him the God of Theater. Oh, Caryl
Churchill, big — whose agent are you? *(Beat. He listens briefly.)* Fine,
that's fine, I understand your point but you need to understand, I'm
forty years old and I've done the work that one is supposed to do to
get one's self to the point that one is supposed to get to, where one
doesn't have to audition anymore. I've gotten the reviews, I've gotten the awards, and not only that, I have the pedigree, my father has
a fucking Nobel Prize, I'm a leading man now, I look fantastic, I'm
funny, I'm the guy everybody supposedly wants and I still have to
audition? For the opportunity to play a part that's going to pay me
three hundred dollars a week? Are you joking? No really, are you joking? *(There is a longer pause while he listens to his agent lecture him.)*
Oh, Sam, God, I understand, on a financial level, why I should
have taken that sitcom; God knows the money part makes complete
sense. But legitimacy? It would have made me more *legitimate?* Could
you — I don't — I have to go now. No. Good-bye. Apparently, I
am not yet "A" list. This from *my* agent, a person who works for me,
and who *I* pay. What time is it? Would it be bad for me to have a
drink at nine in the morning?

Buying Time
Michael Weller

Dramatic

Ben (thirties to forties)

> *Ben is a successful corporate lawyer. He is talking to his fellow partners about a problematic case the firm has been working on.*

BEN: It's no use. I spent all weekend on a speech defending Grayhawk. But standing before you now, esteemed colleagues, life-long friends who face a very hard choice, I realize I have no case. *(He puts the speech down on his chair and turns back to the meeting.)* Del is right. Keeping Grayhawk makes no sense. We stand to lose major money. Big clients. The income graph someone hung on the back wall even shows us having to close our doors. The risk is unacceptable. So let's find our client a good, high-end firm like D&R, and wish them luck. Of course that firm may have their own Sutter, who dislikes environmental clients. So LivEarth will have to go shopping again. And again. And ultimately they will lose to Reinhardt for lack of skilled counsel. But is that really our problem? Del says no. So the Tuintu Forest will become matchsticks and greeting cards. Why should we try and stop that from happening? Just because we swore to represent LivEarth to the fullest extent of the law? Because we gave our word, each and every one of us, when we interviewed here, to protect Rule 7? Is our word, our oath any reason to risk living at a mere six times the national average instead of ten, because that's the real dimension of the threat, not those four-color charts Del hung in back to scare you. Yes, we're at risk. And that risk, Del says, is unacceptable. It's no reason to defend Grayhawk. *(Pause.)* Unless. Unless. Unless any small corner of us is not for sale. Like what we stand for, our pledge to rule 7, our self-respect, our promise to a client. You see, that's really what's at stake tonight, our faith in who we are. *Time Magazine* called us the brightest point of light on the moral compass of the law today. I always thought D&R was unique. I don't know about you, but that's why *I've* worked here, and not somewhere else, for twenty years. I love the law. I love it with all my heart. *(He controls his tears.)* That's why I chose to practice where what we believe means more than what we earn. If money brings you to the law, there's no end of firms ready to welcome you with open arms. Apply, name your price, be happy. But get the hell out of *my* firm. Because here, we honor our legal obligation to every client who walks through the door, even when it's dangerous. Because, god damn it, *here* that is who *we* are. That is what *we* do. If you don't like it, if you feel as Del does, you don't belong here. Get out. But if you believe in what we represent, vote for Grayhawk. If we win tonight, I promise you, the greatest days of Donne & Russo lie ahead.

Buying Time
Michael Weller

Dramatic

Max (thirties to forties)

Max is a partner in a law firm. He's talking to some other lawyers in the firm about how he came to work there.

MAX: I came to Mesa to get laid, d'I ever tell you? True story, and not a word of this to Maia, cause we were already engaged. I had this job interview in Frisco, and an old girlfriend from law school calls, "Hey, Maxie, drive through Mesa on your way west, and we'll get it on."

So we're in bed getting biological, and she starts in about this place where she's a summer associate; D&R, some little weird-ass firm that *pays* you for pro bono work, up to 20 percent of billable hours, and it's in the fuckin' *bylaws,* Rule 7 it's called, and I'm going "This chick is stoned, what's she talking about, legal aid or something" — she's grabbing my hand, putting it places but I'm getting curious about this firm of hers, like "Who pays for these free hours?" and she's going "Harder Max, faster," but I'm very interested now, like "How does it work, the rainmakers subsidize the freebies, and they're *okay* with this?" She's making these moany-gurgling noises but now I'm going nuts trying to work it out; I mean, are these guys for-real grown-up attorneys, or are we talking Larry-the-Lawyer wanna-bees who passed their bar exam after five tries? So next morning I swing by the place to check it out, and hallelujah! Everything she said was true. It was legal paradise, man. I applied on the spot.

Chagrin Falls
Mia McCullough

Dramatic

Riley (fifties)

> *Riley is talking to Patrice, a young Asian-American reporter, about his experiences in the Vietnam War.*

RILEY: No. Patrice, I know . . . I know you probably don't have it in you to understand. That you can't know what it's like to be this stupid farm boy, sent to this foreign place, and ordered to kill people you ain't got nothing against. What it's like to be so homesick that your bones ache, and your nerves are shot from explosions going off all the time, and you can't close your eyes because the things you've seen come to you when you close your eyes. So you go to a bar with the guys to drink away your pain and your fear. And you sit in the corner 'cause you don't feel like talkin' and laughin' and pretendin' there's no war outside. And this waitress comes up to you and when you look up at her it's like she can see right inside you. And suddenly you know scared must look the same no matter what language you speak, because she can see how scared you are. And just when you feel your eyes start to water and you're about to come apart, she puts her tiny little hand on your arm and squeezes. And somehow that little gesture, those little hands, they hold you together and keep you from crumbling. You can't believe how strong she is, that she can hold you together like that. And you wait for her every night. You wait for her to get off work so you can walk her home. So she can hold your hand and keep you whole. 'Cause all you need to survive this place, this war, this world, is to know there's a little bit of kindness out there . . . and then they tell you you're being moved out to some other place with a name you can't pronounce and you go to say goodbye to her. And she already knows somehow, and she looks afraid for the first time. And she's saying something to you that you can't understand. But you know it's important. You can see on her face that it's urgent that you know. And while you're standing there looking at her like an idiot with tears running down your face, she takes your hands and presses them on her belly . . . And it's like she's punched you in the gut. It's all joy and horror and confusion. And you hold her and you cry and you kiss her good-bye and you never see her again . . . You look so much like her . . . But she'd be twenty-eight now . . . If it was a girl.

Chagrin Falls
Mia McCullough

Dramatic

Thaddeus (twenties)

> *Thaddeus, a young man in his twenties, is talking to Patrice, a young Asian-American reporter of about the same age.*

THADDEUS: You don't need to say anything. Everyone knows. You can't have a bad haircut in this town without the whole fuckin' world knowing about it. I'm sure Irene and I are a regular topic of conversation at the ladies' bridge club and the Moose Lodge . . . That's why I hate this fucking place. There's no privacy. There's not a person in this town that doesn't know that I got this scar when Roger Delford beat me to a pulp in the fifth grade, or that Riley spent close to a year in a mental hospital after he came back from the war, or that Henry Harcourt was born with a misshapen head and his brother Tom mushed it back into proper shape when no one was lookin'. It's like you're constantly dragging your past around with you in this town, having your mistakes on display. And then you come along, asking me all these questions and all the sudden I'm talking about myself for nearly the first time in my entire life. And I'm telling you about me. Not about the way everyone else sees me, but about how I see me. And I'm leaving things out, because you don't have to know that I didn't kiss a girl until I was eighteen, and that the girl was old enough to be my mother. That she was best friends with my mother. You don't have to know that the whole town snickers behind my back because I'm screwing the barkeep who's past her prime. But now you know. Now you're just another person I can't look in the eye.

It's just . . . She's the only one who really understands how it's been for me with my mom sick. It's bad enough that they all think of me as the freak-boy with the books. And now that I've been with Irene, none of the other girls will look twice at me, not that they did before. Not that any of 'em have half a brain in their heads. I don't know why I'm telling you this. It's like you opened up some kind of floodgate in me the other day and now I can't shut up.

Chagrin Falls

Mia McCullough

Dramatic

Riley (fifties)

> *Riley is talking to Patrice, a young Asian-American reporter visiting his town for an execution, about the effect the execution, and the crime that necessitated it, has had on the town.*

RILEY: . . . It's just been pressin' down on me these past couple-a months since Alice died. This whole death thing. I've been tryin' to make sense of it. Trying to make sense of what I've done with my life. Fightin' in a war, makin' a livin'. I've always been killing things. I ain't never been in the prison, but I've been thinking a lot about this Jonas fella, this past week and whoever's got to kill him. We got some shitty jobs, the lot of us. Americans eat more beef than any other nation in the world and how many people kill cows? A few thousand? We got how many people on death row? Hundreds? And how many folks who got to put the needle in their arm? Maybe thirty? I'm not sayin' the act itself is wrong. We got to eat. We got to protect ourselves. If we were a tribe, we'd all be hunting, killing our own food. And if there were someone like Jonas who went around raping and murdering little girls, we'd have to execute him. We couldn't just exile him and have him lurkin' around. We couldn't waste able-bodied men to keep him captive when we need them hunting and working in the fields, right? We'd have to kill him to protect the tribe. It'd be the only reasonable thing. But now we got a whole nation of people and everybody's got their job. Some people make shoes, some people push paper, some people keep men in cages and some people kill cows. And pigs and chickens and other people. I mean, I know we got to do it, but it doesn't seem right that the dirty work should rest on so few shoulders, you know? . . . I don't think the human soul was made to stand it all. All that grief. I know mine wasn't.

The Crumple Zone
Buddy Thomas

Comic

Terry (twenties to thirties)

Terry is a flamboyant, hyper gay guy. He is talking to Matt, another gay man, a friend.

TERRY: I noticed all this crap cause I was walking really slow, you know, to Buck's office. What the hell was I doin there, anyway? I shouldn't be there, it's not my business, I should be out finding my own soap opera to star in, where I play the lead and I get the trauma and the drama and the long stem rose on Valentine's Day . . . who am I to go in here and tell these boys to cease and desist. It's NONE OF MY BUSINESS. So, I'm walking really slow, through this car expo, ya know, thinkin about what to say, or should I just go home, and all of a sudden, I'm at this big gigantic exhibit right in the middle of the mall. It's a car, right, with two crash-test dummies in the front seat. And it's one of those things, like at a theme park, an audio, whatever, animatronical thing that moves. There's this wall, see, a face wall, and the car is on this short little track. So these crash-test dummies, they talk. They say, "Hiya folks! We're gonna show you how the Cougar XR-40 can save your life!" The next thing I know, the car goes flyin into this wall! The front of the car crumples up like an accordion and PA-POOFATAH! This big white air bag inflates in the front seat and saves the dummies from decapitation.

Goin' for the metaphor, babe, stay with me . . . So. So then the little animatronic guy says "Don't be a dummy. Drive safe." And the crowd applauds like if they just saw opening night of *Star Wars*. The air bag deflates, the car uncrumples, and the dummies do the same thing all over again. I stood there watchin it for like fifteen minutes. Crash! Crumple! Air bag! Poof! Like twenty times. This display musta cost a million dollars!

Look it's obvious, I'm not the fuckin Poet Laureate of Staten Island, okay? Uh, it's just you got a choice. We all do. We can sit in the car and get battered 'til our brains fall out, or we can get out before it hits the wall again. It's easy. It's obvious. Life isn't so obvious. Who gives a fuck? Just live and be happy, and try not to get too banged up along the way. Drive safe, babe. Don't be a dummy.

The Crumple Zone
Buddy Thomas

Comic

Alex (twenties to thirties)

> *Alex is a gay man talking to his friends about his experiences as a department-store Santa Claus.*

ALEX: Well, I'm sure she would've if she had a pack handy, but she didn't so she decided instead to spit on me and punch me in the stomach and rip my beard off and run across the mall to the Gap, waving my beard in the air, and luckily, this Gap sales lady sees the whole thing and she grabs it, you know, the beard, and runs back over to the gingerbread house with it, which makes the evil albino girl burst into screaming sobbing tears till all the Gap employees are rushing out to see what the hell is going on, and what's going on is that right at that exact moment, this cutest little kid in the world, five or six years old, little freckles on his nose, little blue cap, little front tooth missing, he comes racing up, and I'm trying to get my knotty, tangled beard back on but the kid doesn't care, he thinks Santa's just havin a bad hair day. He jumps right on my lap. This kid believed. All of a sudden his mother comes clacking up in her Payless pumps and her feathered Frost n' Glow poof-do that hadn't changed a LICK since she got fucked on a beer keg at a frat party in 1985! She grabs my ear in a Lee-Press-On fist and says, "Don't you DARE say you'll bring him a doll!" . . . and she clacks away and stands there like a vulture, Virginia Slim hangin' outa her mouth, kid is totally oblivious to it. Just sits there smilin', bouncin' on my lap. Staten Island Mommie Dearest, blowin' smoke rings in my face. *(Takes a big breath, composes himself:)* The kid is there and I say, "Ho-ho-ho, little boy, what would you like for Christmas? And — okay — ready? What do you think he asks for???

. . . He wants Super Sparkle Barbie Dream Date Deluxe.

What could I tell him? I tell him wouldn't he have more fun with a couple of G.I. Joes?

Not this kid, nooooooo, he wants the one with the pretty dress. So you know what I say? Hey, what else could I say? I say "G.I. Joe looks good in a pretty dress too."

Degas in New Orleans
Rosary O'Neill

Dramatic

Rene Degas (twenties)

> *Rene is the brother of Edgar Degas. He is talking to his sister-in-law, Mathilde.*

> *A two-story rental house on 2306 Esplanade Avenue, New Orleans, Louisiana, 1872. Rene, clutching a baby, enters from the gallery, turns watching the rain. Sips from his flask. Moments later, his sister-in-law Mathilde slips in from the pantry with a bassinet. He turns to her, whispers guiltily, covering his alarm.*

RENE: Did I get the doctor? *(Laughs. Sarcastically.)* In whose boat? There's six feet of water out there. *(Smiles.)* I've been drinking. I've got to have a few drinks to start the day. *(Quietly.)* My wife's bleeding's slowed. But the baby is worse. *(Moved despite himself— helplessly.)* Doctor doesn't want Tell to get too attached, because it's a matter of time. They sent me here to get the baby. I'll take it quick before she comes back. *(With a hurt, bitter look, blinking back tears.)* How tiny, how warm. Poor little creature can't survive long. Struggling to breathe. Oh my God. I'd like to help it — comfort Tell, but — I never wanted this baby, and she knew it. Her name's Jeanne, but she's no fighter. She hardly opens her eyes. When I put my finger in her fist, she barely squeezes. I rub her stomach, but she hardly notices. *(A look of terror comes into his eyes.)* If only I'd acted enthusiastic, gotten more loans through Edgar, things would have turned out all right — *(Wisely.)* Maybe not. *(He winces — all life seeming to drain from his face.)* They say with Jeanne's pneumonia it'll be a sweet painless end. It'll get harder for her to breathe until she stops. I hope I don't have to see it. My wife doesn't know. *(He stammers wearily.)* I had to fake some slight hope for her. *(His eyes look up, defensively.)*

What else could I do? The woman keeps waiting for good news. *(Uneasy now — with alcoholic talkativeness.)* How did this happen? Yesterday I was a banker's son in Paris. Women sparkled about me, sent me perfumed notes, anonymous flowers. I thought I'd come to Louisiana and Tell's father would make me a southern planter. Louisiana was the New World. Where you could be a success by age thirty. Yesterday I was a superficial dreamer. That was the real me. *(Looks down at the infant. He sighs gloomily and resentfully.)* I tried, swear to God. What did I find when I got here? Lazy people too lost to help me. Mosquitoes, moths, and caterpillars dropping from trees. A bitter humidity, thousand-leg spiders, termites gobbling all they see. Prehistoric roaches. A stifling heat. A river waiting to burst its banks full of alligators and moccasins, and water rats fleeing up the oak trees. Children dropping with yellow fever, scarlet fever, typhoid. Unnamed infections. Hurricanes, floods, and infants struggling to breathe. *(In a changed tone — repentantly.)* I suppose I'll order a little casket. *(Gulps from a flask, grins wryly.)* Thank God for alcohol. Things seem pinker, calmer. A strange quiet soothes your ears, making you able to hear anything, accept anything. *(With drunken melancholy.)* Soon in a room of death you are peacefully alone. *(Rene holds up the flask, then walks out heavily.)*

Drift
Jon Tuttle

Comic

Lee (thirties to fifties)

> *Lee is a wisecracking, cynical private investigator. In this monologue, he's talking to some other guys in a bar about his views on marriage.*

LEE: I don't know. Being married. It's like . . . it's like chewing the same damn gum *over* and *over* for the *rest* of your *life*. Sometimes, sometimes you need some new gum.

Some Juicy Fruit. Huh? Some *Bazooka!* Boom, pow! Fidelity, hey, for my money: I'm all for it. But it's not the same thing as *monogamy.* This is a common mistake. Monogamy — is *demeaning,* it's an imposition on *nature.* Nature abhors a wedding. It's *blackmail,* the whole thing. And that's all it is. And they work it so the only fuckin' thing harder'n bein' married is gettin' divorced. Know how easy it is to get a divorce in Egypt? You walk up to her, you say, "I divorce thee, I divorce thee, I divorce thee." Three times: boom.

That was like, in olden times. Tijuana, you get a divorce for what, fifty bucks. Here? *Christ.* It's easier to fake your own *death.* My wife, we litigated like *wolverines* . . . You think you know somebody? You say you're *married* to her, you *live* with her? So *what.* You divorce somebody, you see shit you never seen before. *(Pause. Lee drinks, remembers:)* . . . People are vicious fucks. You know? People are savage, flesh-eating vicious fucks. . . . And I have a high opinion of people.

Father's Shadow
Elvira Carrizal

Dramatic

Señor Gomez (late forties to early fifties)

> *Señor Gomez, a Mexican-American man is talking to Javier, his son-in-law, and is referring to his daughter, Sonya.*

SEÑOR GOMEZ: Look at her, son. I told you she wouldn't be a good wife. She wasn't ready. You should have let me finish doing my job and then you could have married her, but you thought you were so smart. You were too impatient. There were other ways to fulfill those urges. You're a man and women are easy to find, but a good wife . . . a good wife takes time. Look at my wife. After her first husband died, she came to me. She needed someone to take care of her and Sonya. It's a fair trade. We work hard to put a roof over their head and to put food on the table. They thank us by serving us. Except Sonya. She broke tradition and you helped her do it. And now look at what you have done. And all for what? For love! *(Laughs.)* It's a shame you didn't have a man raising you. But that's what happens. Once tradition is broken, everything else goes wrong. Leave her, son. She's not going to change. It's too late. There's nothing you can do. She going to make your life miserable. She's useless. Think about Anthony. You need to raise him right. You need to teach him to be a man.

Five Nickels
Jack Neary

Dramatic

Ed (fifties)

> *Ed is talking to Catherine, a woman who's interested in him, about his mid-life crisis.*

ED: Well . . . it wasn't like now. Back then. That's all. And somebody like me . . . well . . . I thought havin' a girl . . . was more special . . . than maybe it was. I was the oldest, and my father died when I was just a kid and . . . I kind of took his place. So my mother and I married off my brothers and we married off Martha and I was just so . . . I worried so much about them finding their special people . . . that I never thought a lot about finding one myself . . . Oh, I had a lot of friends that were girls . . . *(Smiles.)* . . . and they knew . . . they knew where O'Connor was gettin' his material. But that was different. It wasn't like today. There was more . . . respect. There was more . . . I don't know. Whatever it was, there was more. Today I look around at the kids and this one's in the drugstore buyin' condoms and that one's havin' babies in high school and the other one's livin' with . . . I don't know . . . her significant brother or whatever the hell they call it. Doesn't seem natural today to . . . to be on your own. To just . . . wait. But that's what I did. I kept . . . waitin'. Now, sometimes, I think maybe I blew it. Maybe I let life pass me by. But, then, no, I say to myself . . . I'm still the same person I was at forty, when I was still the same person I was at twenty, who was still the same person I turned into when my father died and I started . . . waitin'. And that's all right. I think. I try not to kick myself about it anymore.

Five Nickels
Jack Neary

Dramatic

Ed (fifties)

> *Ed is talking to Catherine, a woman who's interested in him, about why he would be no good for her.*

ED: *(Thinks a moment.)* I wanted to tell her that I thought she was the prettiest girl I'd ever seen in my life. That's the prettiest girl in town, the prettiest girl in the movies, the prettiest girl in the magazines. The prettiest girl anywhere. Any time. And I wanted to tell her how beautiful I thought it was that she could be so pretty and so . . . pleasant at the same time. I wanted to thank her for laughing at my jokes, and for visiting my mother in the hospital every day for three months, and then staying by me all through the wake and the funeral. I wanted to tell her that whatever love was, she had to be it. I wanted to tell her that I wish there were two of her, because I knew she belonged to my best friend. And, God help me, I wanted to tell her that nobody was ever gonna take her place in my heart. That's what I wanted to tell her. And that's what I put down in the couple of letters I wrote and never sent. And that's why I think I've wasted all but fourteen years of my life. And that's why I think you can do a whole lot better than me.

Force Continuum
Kia Corthron

Dramatic

Dece (twenties to thirties)

Dece, a black, off-duty cop, is talking to the bartender in a bar.

DECE: Ten:thirty-four domestic, nutcase wavin' a hammer around wife under the table, we ready for whatever we gotta. He give it up, sobbin'. Her with a black eye, arm all limp all wrong. Broke. But got hers in, side a his face cut and bloody. Razor. So she file the charges we bring him in, overnight in the tank she come see him, He: "Sorry baby sorry," She: "Sorry honey," weepin', weepin', *then,* to us, ones who save her life: "Why you take my honey away?" THEN wanna file a complaint, say *we* done his cuts, injury in custody, crazy people! Remember? *(The last to Flip. Flip nods not looking at Dece, drinks.)* I'm a kid, this cop knew my dad, comes by our house, Christmas drink. Says his partner in a mess, plainclothes the late tour, Harlem, bastard puts a knife to his throat, cop kills the guy. Now usually everybody on the block see no evil, hear no evil but *some*how, *some*how word leaked *this* shootin' a *police* shootin', victim black. Cop black too but that meant nothin', this shot fired at four in the mornin' *no*body around but suddenly a hundred witnesses and guess what word on everyone's lips: *brutality. (Dece drinks, notices bartender looking at him.)* WHAT? You got somethin' to ask? Like am I black or am I cop?

Force Continuum
Kia Corthron

Dramatic

Father (fifties)

> *Father, a black man in his fifties and a cop, is talking to his father, a
> retired policeman, about the anguish he experiences every day on the job.*

FATHER: I done my job! I done my job can't no one say I ain't done my
badass job *I*'m the one! *most* hated, black one, traitor. When they
scream "Murderer!" the spit come out with it which we s'posed to
assume is involuntary, who get the bulk of it? *Me. (Pacing.)* Nigger
this nigger that I hear their shit, comments, over the radio, in the
squadroom, "monkeys," "jungle" I do my thing can't no one say I
ain't. *(Mocking.)* "How can you respect these people when they don't
respect themselves?" FUCK them. Cops, not the first time! I seen it
before I try to calm 'em down, *animals*, try to put on their brakes,
bastards and they start their suspicions, 'm I parta the team? Cuz when
the goin' get rough they got my back, someone come up on me from
behind they's who I depend on 'M I PARTA THE TEAM? *White
cops* 'M I parta the team? This time . . . They thought I wouldn't do
it, join in dumb punk, perp dumb kid. Why he gotta have such a
smart mouth? What his mama teach him. I kick him! Fuck them
they got the controls: promotions, assignments they control it. I *better* be a buddy! Promotions which I seen *nothin'* of so far, *nothin'*,
trouble passin' the written test but others ain't passed made it, "dis-
cretion a the Department" cronyism! And a little too dark to be a
crony, only thing not dark about me's my shield, white shield. They
white shield me forever How about now? I make grade *now?* Detective
now? Think we soft they always thinkin' we soft on our own. Think
niggers helpin' niggers "These people," "These people" Fuck them!
Fuck Arty fuck 'em! *All! (Silence.)*

God Rest Ye Merry Gentlemen

Don Nigro

Comic

McDuffy (elderly)

> *McDuffy is an elderly English actor/manager who tours with his own
> small company, playing English backwaters. Here he is talking to Mary
> Margaret, brought to him by his former protégé John Rose, who is try-
> ing to save her from a self-destructive downward spiral. John Rose thinks
> McDuffy can straighten her out.*

MCDUFFY: You ARE nobody. You're an actor. An actor is nobody. That's
his job. Everybody is nobody and an actor is nobody who knows he's
nobody and chooses the gloriously foolish role of one who takes on
the identity of that which he is not and in doing so, in performing
this thankless and absurd act of love, this shared identity with another being, the fusion of his nobody with this imaginary creature
who never was, this unholy union of identities creates the illusion
of meaning, the illusion, if done at all well, of purpose and signifi-
cance, and this does enable somehow the continuance and sharing
of experience which is courage which is truth which is love which is
the only damned thing we have or anybody has or ever will have.
And I think it's just remotely possible that you can do that. But instead, blessed absurdly with this unspeakably fragile and infinitely
precious opportunity, you pee in your pants and scurry away like a
little mouse, because your precious feelings are much too tender, because you don't want me judging you? You would give up the chance
to do this noble, extraordinary thing because you're afraid, you ridiculous, pathetic, ignorant little twat?

God Rest Ye Merry Gentlemen
Don Nigro

Dramatic

John Rose (forties)

> *John Rose is an American actor who has left film stardom in the 1920s to return to his roots in the English theater. He has returned to the seedy company that gave him his start with Mary Margaret, an alcoholic young American actress wannabe, whom he is trying to save and to whom he is speaking here.*

JOHN ROSE: Wait a minute. Will you just wait? Look. When you and I met — you weren't the only one just about at the end of their rope. I've spent my life running away. I've abandoned my family, I've abandoned Mac and this company more than once. It's true he's not always heaven to work with, and some of it was his fault, but most of it was mine. It was inside me. I've run away from every good thing that's happened to me. When I get to feeling too close, I run away. To the war. To the movies. It's something I do. Experience has taught me that committing yourself to anything real is either impossible or fatal, either to you or somebody you love. Most of my life has been lies. My father wasn't really the person they said was my father. I have a child somewhere I can never acknowledge is mine. I've burned just about every bridge I could find. When I found you, you were as lost as I was. You were miserable and alone and you weren't sure you wanted to live any more. And I looked at you and I said to myself, this is a situation you can actually do something about. This is somebody who could be happy if she just had a reason to be. And maybe I needed a reason to come back here, or something I could tell myself was the reason, when the real reason was that I missed these people and this work so desperately I thought I was going to go insane. It's hard to go back to people you've betrayed. But I could come back because I was bringing you, and I knew it was the right thing. I knew you could do this, that you could belong here. And if you could belong here, then maybe there was a chance I could, too, despite everything. But I knew if I — I didn't want it to turn into just another — because it wasn't just another — I wanted to do the right thing, for once, for somebody, for you. And I was afraid.

House of Trash

Trav S. D.

Dramatic

Bob (twenties to forties)

> *Bob is a loquacious garbageman who moonlights as a Baptist preacher.
> Here, he's ranting to Ma, a toothless, tobacco-chewing hag.*

BOB: Hayseed's Pubert done run off with some painty-faced harlot from
the Satan cult.

Hayseed found 'em neckin' and smokin' pot up at the college
when he went up to buy fertilizer. Got so ticked off he hauled off
and whupped Pube, and Pube stole off with this floozy. Twenty-five-
year older, she is. Said she's one of these Goths like on *20/20* and a
dead ringer for Marilyn Manson. Tattooed from head to toe like a
Freejee cannibal, with an earring on her lip, and pentygrams like polka
dots on a clown's overcoat.

Five-pointed emblem of the Satanic cult people. Steal children
from kindergartens, rape 'em, and then erase their memory so they
think nothin' ever happened. For all I know it happened to me.
(Shudders.) Diabolical! Hayseed ain't liftin' a finger to save that boy's
soul. He's up to his elbows in that goat of his. You'd think he'd pull
his hand out his ass for two seconds and listen to the word of God.
Communication. That's what it is. That's what I'm always telling the
families down at the parish. You don't have trust in a family. Something's gone bust. Pubert may have felt he had something he needed
to talk about, but he felt he couldn't bring it up, he couldn't discuss
it with his father. So he went off and did his own dirty thing anyway. See what I mean? Communication.

House of Trash

Trav S. D.

Dramatic

Bob (twenties to forties)

Bob is a garbageman who moonlights as a Baptist preacher. He's talking to Toby, an alienated skinhead teen.

BOB: Oh, I can see the whole thing, in living color. Drunk on Wild Turkey. So blind drunk he can hardly stand. High on that coke, too. The two of them. Out of their minds, insensible — reckless. So much so that they stop off at Grandpa's, one door over from Hayseed's farm so they can go for a roll in the hay, so doped up they can't hardly stand. That hayloft air — I know it. It's like another drug itself. Thick, sweet, hot, moist. Goes right to the head. Sure, I remember. Your eyes get watery and irritated up there. Your nostrils get greedy for it, open right up wide. Skin gets all flushed, excited. And it's hot up there in that hayloft! Hundred and five degrees. You work up a sweat not doin' nothin'. Just standin' there. Just standin' there not doin' nothin'. Just talkin'. Talkin' about nothin'. So you're not doin' nothing, just standin' there not doin' nothin' and ya ain't talkin' about nothing. Just nothin'. That's all yer talkin' about. Nothin'! It's a game you play, the two of ya. Neither one's thinkin' about the words. Just waitin' to see how it'll happen. Who'll hop on who. Heart's just thumpin', man. Like there's a little guy bangin' on the inside of your chest, yellin' "Let me out!" And the two of you, you're drunk on Wild Turkey, so you just gotta kinda stumble into her, and the two of you, you just go, tumblin' gentle into the hay, laughing and kissin' them whiskey-flavored kisses. That's how it happens. Bury your face in her sweaty neck there, and just kinda sloppily slidin' your mouth up and down from her ear to her shoulder. Just like eatin' watermelon. Once you get down on that shoulder, boy, why it's only a matter of time afore she unbuttons her damn shirt herself. You don't have to do a thing, don't have to think about a thing. Your body does the whole trick itself. Your mind don't have to move a muscle. Soon her jeans are slidin' down them sweaty slim legs, boy. By God, she's a woman, boy! WHHOOOOEEEEE! YEAH! Lookee thar! Hell! She don't have to tell you twice. When you're eighteen, there ain't no amount of whiskey gonna make Johnny fall down. So you git on in there and ya, ya DO YER BIDNESS! YES, SIR!!!

House of Trash

Trav S. D.

Dramatic

Toby (teens)

> *Toby is an alienated skinhead teen with a thing for Babe, a trucker's wife, to whom he is talking.*

TOBY: I think you deserve better than that.

Like, I dunno. Somebody new. Someone whose body's not riddled with liver spots, whose chest doesn't rattle when he breathes, whose nerves haven't been shot through drugs and drink. A man who can read the warning label on a bottle of Drano and do simple sums without frowning. Someone who's not a disgusting swine unfit to wash the shit out of your underwear like Ray is. *(Steps into spotlight.)* You need a man . . . a boy, really . . . perhaps the only person you can really talk to in this whole town. Someone who tried to understand your grown-up problems from his limited vantage point at your feet. Someone who's sat in the front row just so he wouldn't have to squint to stare at you. Who's learned more from the husky warm buzz of your voice and flutter of your eyelids than all textbook assignments put together. Who's traced the contour of your neck, the base of your jaw, your slender shoulders again and again until he memorized you, could do a sculpture of you. Who would only bring you flowers but he knows that they're mere piss to your perfume. Who would learn to play the harp for you if you decided you liked music. Who would powder the ground before you as you walked with the pulverized bones of royalty. Who would exterminate the world at your whim. Who would raze the holy temples to make you a home. Who would club baby harp seals to make you a coat. Who hates the world, hates everything, but loves you, adores you, needs you and everything you stand for, everything you represent. Who would die for you, KILL for you. Someone like . . . like . . . that.

House of Trash
Trav S. D.

Dramatic

Bob (twenties to forties)

> *Bob is a garbageman who moonlights as a Baptist preacher. He's talking to a farmer named Hayseed in this outrageous rant.*

BOB: They're awful unjust to the poor white man in this country, Hayseed. It's the last socially acceptable prejudice. We're the butt of scorn of every other American faction and called names you wouldn't call the dog that ate your baby. Cracker, redneck, peckerwood, slackjaw, yokel, white trash — Trash! As though a man were a potato peel, a candy wrapper, a cigar butt. Trash, refuse, garbage, waste, waste! Spilled sperm, bottom feeders, cannon fodder. My people come over to this country 300 years ago as indentured servants — practically slaves — and since then we've been sharecroppers, miners, factory workers, gas station attendants and groundskeepers, the people who clean the pools and ring up the groceries. I come that close to paying the black man's dues in this country and still they're all railroaded into thinking I'm capable of oppressing anybody. It's like blaming Tom Joad for the sins of Henry Ford. You gotta have power to oppress somebody! Ted Turner and Ted Kennedy, all the pretty privileged Teds, are slapping each other's knees red over that one. Couple of fat cats buffalo the people into thinking they're saints and make me out to be a rodeo clown. Now Roseanne's our Aunt Jemima and Jeff Foxworthy's our Uncle Tom. Somewhere, somehow, someone's probably laughing at me right now. But I haul your garbage. Your garbage. A hair away from wiping your ass without a glove. You oughtta give me a medal for that. Instead that just makes you all the more contemptuous of me, as though I deserve it somehow. I oughtta burn your house down for that. Instead, I seek to practice Christian forgiveness, becoming the butt of your jokes for yet another reason.

Everybody's whipping boy. Everybody's scapegoat. And that's all anyone knows about a scapegoat. Is kill the scapegoat. Kill the scapegoat.

The sacrificial lamb to appease an angry God, boy. Cut your losses and buy a little more time. Abraham, a knife and his first-born son. God says you do it and you do it. But sometimes it ain't God that tells ya, just your own craven needs of the moment. Smoke and mirrors. Ya wanna shield yourself from consequences so you kill a scapegoat.

An Irish Play
Dan O'Brien

Dramatic

Declan (twenties)

Declan is an Irish actor rehearsing an Irish play.

DECLAN: WILL PEOPLE STOP TELLING ME TO SIT DOWN!
(Pause.) I will sit down when I choose to sit down, and not a sec-
ond sooner! — Are you angry?

Are you angry? Do you have anything to be angry about? You
have to be angry if you want to kill Brian Boru. You have to be right
awful ferocious to want to murder the Emperor of the Irish, and let
me tell you something, "Joachim Sampson" — if that is your real
name, and I haven't yet made up my mind on the issue of your du-
bious origins — I hate Ireland more than I hate my own life! And
that's saying a lot. I hate Ireland so much I want to drop napalm on
Dingle. I want to queue up Catholic priests and nuns, Irish mothers and fathers, and I want to shoot them, one by one, right between
their Pope-fearing eyes. And then I want to burn them on a barge
floating off Belfast where no will smell the difference. . . . What do
you have to be angry about? You come over here and you take our
jobs and you marry our nice freckled ginger girls. And at night, when
you're lying in bed with her, some of us unlucky sots have no place
to go but here, and then it's home to our refrigerators and our cocks
and our contraband *Playboy* magazines. . . . You're not even Irish,
for fuck's sake! Who invited you to this country — ?

An Irish Play
Dan O'Brien

Dramatic

Ed (forties)

Ed is the director of an Irish play. He is talking to his actors.

ED: Bullocks! I've got no wife, no girl — only half a son . . . I'm doing my best, and I don't need some old drunk with a suicide for a son telling me how to raise my boy. *(Silence.)* Do you know what I do all day? For work? I stand in my office above the cinema, with the pigeon shite across the windows and no furniture, and I wait for the phone to ring. For somebody to ask me to come and measure their emissions. Here I am with my fucking cigarettes, puffing a pack an hour, and I'm supposed to go out and measure other people's pollution? Gas leaks, carbon monoxide, plutonium, radon . . . What the fuck is radon? Can somebody tell me just what this radon is all about? I don't think we really have it in this country, it's something the Americans invented, but I cash in on it all the same. I have to. Child support — another American invention, thank you. Some poor langer out in Ballincollig with latex on everything asks me: "Is it bad, Mr. Deevey?" And I say, "Dr. Deevey to you, and yes, I'm afraid it is bad. Very bad." "What is it then?" they ask — "What is it that's been poisoning my family while they sleep?" "It's whatchacallit. It's the, the Thing. RADON." . . . Jesus. I charge them three hundred quid just to tell them it's radon. They're always thanking me for saving their lives when I go. *(Silence.)*

Jesus Hopped the A Train
Stephen Adly Guirgis

Dramatic

Valdez (thirties to forties)

> *Valdez is an Hispanic prison guard. This is a direct address to the audience.*

VALDEZ: I know an ex-con who did seven years for murdering a nice hot dog vendor. He slept soundly every night, undisturbed by his conscience. He now lives at Gun Hill Road in the Bronx, so, beware if you happen to be around that area. He has no regard for human life, including his own. I would like to take his late-model Sports Utility Vehicle and drive it through his front door, accelerate past his bathroom, and come to a violent, crashing halt right on top of his head, but . . . the law prohibits me. Instead, I simply wish that he dies soon and painfully . . . Whenevah I see him, I say, "I wish you die soon and painfully" . . . Before I became a Corrections Officer, I worked for the Department of Sanitation hauling garbage. It used to amaze me, the valuable items people would cavalierly discard. It angered me. Couches, alarm-clock radios, family photos. I often wanted to go to people's apartments and throttle them. One time I saw a guy throw out a very nice color television set. I asked him if it still worked. He said "Yes." I asked him why he didn't just give it away instead of trashing it. He smirked at me. I slapped him. People think everything is replaceable. Everything is not replaceable. People believe they go through life accumulating things. That is incorrect. People go though life discarding things, tangible and intangible, replaceable and priceless. What people do not understand is that once they have discarded an irreplaceable item, it is lost forever . . . *(Blackout.)*

Jesus Hopped the A Train
Stephen Adly Guirgis

Dramatic

Angel (twenties)

> *Angel is a young Hispanic man being held in Riker's Island prison await-*
> *ing trial for murdering a cult religious leader. Here he is talking to his*
> *court-appointed attorney.*

ANGEL: You got any friends, Mary Jane?! 'Cuz we gotta friend, Eustace,
he's doin life in Arizona, but we stopped hangin' wit him when we
was like eleven! And we got this other friend, Crazy Legs, he died a
cancer at twenty-two, and dass hard, but, at least he's dead! At least
we could account for him, ya know? We'd go to the park, Grant's
Tomb, smoke a joint, we'd save the last hit for Crazy Legs, put the
roach to the side. Or playin. Chinese handball, you know, with the
boxes?

When we'd play, don't matter how many people we got, the last
box is for Lindsay Fernandez who can't play no more —

Wheelchair, he ain't around, but again, at least I know why he's
not around. But Joey? He juss gone. Bang: out! It'd be one thing if
he was out for some good reason, like if he was an astronaut in space
chasin the cure for AIDS, but what he out for? He out for bullshit!
He out 'cuz Reverend Kim sold him a phony bill a goods —

Do you know what Reverend Kim say? He say he's the Son of
God! I mean, how big does your fuckin' balls have to be to sit there
with a straight face and claim some shit like that? Son a God???!! Yo,
even if there was a Son of God, which, I mean, get real — but, ah-
aight, I'm a put it like this: If there was "another" Son of God runnin' around here, juss pickin' up where his older brother left off, tryin'
ta save our ass: He sure as shit ain't Reverend Kim! How many Sons
of God you know drive a Lexus? Or got million dollar stock port-
folios? Or go skiing in Aspen? 'Cuz I'll tell you right now: If Jesus
Christ existed, and I ain't sayin' he did, but if, by some miracle he
actually did, *the mothafuckah didn't ski!!*

Jesus Hopped the A Train
Stephen Adly Guirgis

Dramatic

Angel (twenties)

> *Angel is a young Hispanic man held in Riker's Island prison awaiting trial for murder. He is talking to his court-appointed attorney.*

ANGEL: My friend Joey should be doing what you're doing! He should be a public defender, or a drug counselor, helpin' the people, fuckin' whatever! But where is he? He's out! Gone! And why? Why is he not here? Why? Do you believe that Reverend Kim with his money and his power and his sports cars — do you believe that he's the actual Son of God??! That a man deported from his own country and convicted of tax evasion in this one could even speak for God, let alone be God? That a man who steals people, has them selling flowers on the street, getting rich off them, what the fuck?, look me in my eye and tell me that a man like that should be allowed to do what he's doing without fear of reprisal! With a fuckin' government-approved tax-exempt status and a full police escort?!

Where's my mother's full police escort when she gets off the subway from work after midnight and has to walk home alone? Where's Mother Teresa's Lexus? And how 'bout you? You a public defender, and if you're any good at lawyering at all, you could prolly make a lot more money working someplace else, right? But you don't do that, do you? So where's your mansion? Where's your frappacino, swimming pool, mistress, Son-a-God fuckin' wonderland, huh?! He stole my friend. I shot him in the ass. Now I'm fucked in jail, and he's eating banana crème pie in some plush hospital bed. Juss like the chairman of Philip Morris! Your Pops, he six feet under, fuckin' maggot food now. Where's the Chairman? I'll tell you where the fuckin' chairman is! Out there on the eighteenth green sippin' a Heineken, wiping the crumbs from the shrimp salad sandwich off of his cashmere sweater, and he's smiling.

Jesus Hopped the A Train
Stephen Adly Guirgis

Dramatic

Valdez (thirties to forties)

> *Valdez, a prison guard, is talking to Lucius, an inmate and serial killer
> who has found God in prison.*

VALDEZ: "Saved"?! I am a good man because I choose to be! End of story!
Not because I fear God. Not because I wanna go to some holy play-
ground when I kick the bucket! I go to work, I pay my taxes, I ob-
serve the law. I didn't kill eight people! I don't need to be "saved."
Do you really believe that there's a thing called God? . . . Or is it
that your pain is so unbearable that you force yourself to create a
belief in order to medicate that pain? . . . And, if there is a God,
Superstar, do you honestly believe that you are free from the burden
of what you've done? . . . And if there isn't a God, then what are you
really? In a meaningless existence, your only function was to be a
source of pain and death, like cancer or a plane crash! You renounced
your humanity when you claimed your first victim! Now what are you?
I think you know, Superstar. I look at you, and I know that you know!
And the most compassionate advice I can give you is this: When you
get back to your cell, bang your head against the wall until your brains
spill out, only, please, do it after six so I don't have ta clean the shit
up! . . . Now I will be back . . . shortly! *(Valdez exits.)*

Jesus Hopped the A Train
Stephen Adly Guirgis

Dramatic

Angel (twenties)

> *Angel is a young Hispanic man held in Riker's Island prison awaiting
> trial for murder. He is talking to his court-appointed attorney.*

ANGEL: . . . We usta, me and Joey, we usta sneak out our house on Sunday nights, jump the turnstiles. And we would hop down onto the
subway tracks, walk through the tunnels, lookin' for shit, makin' ad-
ventures, playin' like we was G.I. Joes . . . Pick up a empty can a
Hawaiian Punch or some ol' beer bottle for fake walkie-talkies . . .
and we'd have our snow-boots on so we could be astronauts. And we
would pretend we were the last two survivors on earth and that we
came from the future . . . stupid . . . the future . . . like in that *Planet
of the Apes* movie with the two guys? Only we had no weapons, juss
chocolate milk . . . And we'd get so lost in our games and our dis-
coveries and our made-up stories . . . so many stories: lookin' for ghosts,
lookin' for apes, lookin' for fortunes, runnin' from rats, talkin' bout
girls, talkin' bout Thelma from "Good Times," talkin' bout daydreams,
talkin' 'bout Bruce Lee versus Evil Knievel, talkin' in words that was-
n't even words, . . . and . . . and it would always surprise us when we
saw the Lights . . . even though we could feel the train coming, but
it was the Lights . . . The closer those Lights came, rumble of the tracks,
sound a the conductor's horn blarin' at us. We'd get so excited we'd
freeze — two seconds of freezin' cold . . . hypnotized . . . holdin' hands,
waitin', waitin', then: Bang . . . We'd jump off the rails, hug the wall,
climb back up the platform, start runnin', runnin', tearin' ass clear
across town back to Riverside or Cherry Park . . . One time . . . one
particular time, when we was holdin' hands right before we jumped
off the rails, somethin' happened, and we couldn't let go, couldn't un-
tangle ourself from each other, and we were inside that Light, and we

both saw skeletons and radiation, and we was paralyzed in a way that I juss can't explain, till somethin' blew us apart, juss blew us, and we landed safe . . . We didn't move for a long time . . . We was cryin' and Joey ripped his brother's coat . . . We wasn't speakin' till we got to our block and Joey said that it was The Light that ripped us apart and saved our lives . . . Joey said, "Jesus hopped the A train to see us safe to bed" . . .

Killer Joe
Tracy Letts

Dramatic

Chris (twenties)

> *Chris, a trailer-trash guy is talking to Joe, a man he and his father have hired to murder his mother for her insurance.*

CHRIS: *(Offstage.)* Joe?! Joe?! *(Chris rushes in, sweating, out of breath, panicked. His head and hand are bruised, bandaged. Joe holsters his gun.)* Ah, thank God! I was afraid . . . I wouldn't get here, and . . . it'd be too late . . . ah, thank God . . . Listen. We gotta stop this thing. We can't . . . *(Chris turns off the radio.)* I been in a lotta trouble, all my life, but I never tried nothin' like this before. I'm sorry. I didn't mean to waste your time. I hate that bitch. I've always hated her. I just . . . I can't be the one, y'know? But more than that, the main thing, really, is, is, is Dottie. I mean, my sister . . . she never did nothin' to nobody, y'know? And for me to . . . I can't be . . . responsible. And you can't have her. I can't let you have her. You gotta give her up, cause I can't look her in the eyes otherwise. Do you understand, Joe? I don't want my sister to see you again. I don't think you're a good influence. I mean, come on, Joe, you kill people, for Chrissake. Y'know? No offense, I mean, it's not like me and Dad or Mom have been especially good influences. But Dottie managed to turn out all right anyway. And it just seems like the best thing I can do for her now is to keep her away from people who won't do her any good. So I think it'd be best if you and me just shook hands and forgot any of us ever met. Is that OK? Can't we walk away from it before it goes too far? None of us are any better off, but we're really no worse off, either. I'm no better off. I owe Digger Soames six thousand dollars. I'll never have that kinda money, not ever. And, you know, even if I had it, wouldn't that suck, handin' it over to these guys? I'd wanna keep that money, try to make somethin' with it. I tried startin' a farm once. That seemed like the kind of life I want. Workin' for myself, outside a lot, make my own hours, live in the country, smoke dope, watch TV. That's all I really want. So I started a rabbit farm, I built the whole thing, by myself. I was livin' with a couple guys out near Mesquite, but they didn't help me; I built it, with my own two hands. Lumber, chicken wire, water bottles, pellets. Rabbits. I loved those little bastards. They smell like shit, and they fuck all the time, but they're awful easygoin' animals. I left for a couple weeks, cause of this girl down in Corpus, and when I got back, a rat, or a skunk, or somethin' had got in the pen, and it was rabid. Awful hot out, too. They just tore each other apart. Their eyes were rollin', and foamin' at the mouth, and . . . and screamin'. Did you know rabbits can scream? They sound just like little girls. It was disturbing. I started sellin' dope for a living. I knew more about it. *(Joe checks a beeper affixed to his belt, then goes to the door, looks outside.)* So I can't pay this guy, and I don't even really want to. That means you gotta get out, Joe. You gotta get outta here, and leave my sister alone forever. Otherwise, you and me're gonna have some trouble. Do you understand? Do you understand?

Lobby Hero
Kenneth Lonergan

Comic

Jeff (twenties)

> *Jeff, a front-desk guard in a luxury apartment building, is talking to William, his supervisor.*

JEFF: *I* only went in the Goddamn Navy to get my old man off my back then suddenly I'm up on charges and I'm out on my ass. My old man won't talk to me, I got no place to live, I bum around like a . . . bum: I gotta move in with my brother Marty, which is totally humiliating. My old man dies, thank God —

— I try to work up a little stake playing poker, I turn around, I got the Goddamn loansharks comin' after me. I gotta borrow five thousand dollars from my brother so I don't get my legs broken. I date this girl, it turns out she's *still* a prostitute only now she only does it "on the side" whatever that means. I break up with her, I'm scared I'm gonna get AIDS, I can't meet anybody

And *then* William, *then*, I come to you, William, and with your beautiful generosity you give me this job, you take a little interest in me, and just look at me now: I just broke up with a nice girl, from a good family, I'm looking around for someone new. I'm payin my own rent to Marty, buyin my own groceries, and I'm a healthy member of the workforce for nine months straight come Friday. And I'll tell you something else, man: My spirit is OK. I don't have a broken spirit. I just want to stick it out here at least a year, so I can really get that under my belt — just for my own — just psychologically.

Yeah, that's what I told myself. At least one year, right? Day shift, night shift, I don't care. But I just started lookin' around for my own place, which'll be the first time I had my own home in six years. My own little living room where I can sit and watch TV: a nice little kitchen I can cook my meals in. Invite a girl over for dinner and be the only one there with her. And William, I owe it all to you. So see? You really helped somebody. Now that might be your good character but it's my good luck.

Lobby Hero
Kenneth Lonergan

Comic

Jeff (twenties)

> *Jeff, a front-desk guard in a luxury apartment building is talking to Dawn, a female rookie cop whom he is sweet on.*

JEFF: Hey, can I ask you something, Officer?

Do you know why the New York City cops changed from the light blue shirts to the dark blue shirts recently? Like a couple of years ago? I'm not sayin like "Do you know" and then like, I tell you the *answer.* I'm really asking, 'cause I thought you might know.

Remember how a long time ago, like when we were kids, the police uniforms used to be all dark blue? And then around the 1980s I guess, they switched them to dark blue pants and a light blue shirt? And then recently they switched 'em back to dark blue pants and a dark blue shirt again? What *I* always wondered was, Did they throw out all the old dark blue pants when they did that or did they just throw out all the light blue shirts and then get dark blue shirts that matched the old dark blue pants, so they wouldn't have to buy all new pants? Because that would be quite a savings.

If you think about it, you could be wearing pants right now that were being worn by some lady cop in 1975, if you think about it. Except I guess the women police officers didn't wear pants back in 1975. I don't mean they didn't wear pants, like they were walkin' around in their underwear. I just mean I think they were still wearin' skirts back then, weren't they? I know I'm blathering, I'm just completely in love with you, can I just say that?

Lobby Hero
Kenneth Lonergan

Comic

Bill (thirties to forties)

Bill, a beat cop, is talking to Jeff, a front-desk guard in a luxury apartment building, about his partner Dawn.

BILL: I see a little girl wearin' a police uniform. OK? I see a little girl from the neighborhood who some moron told her she could be a cop. But she's not a cop right now. But if somebody takes a shot at her, or somebody else's life depends on her, they're not gonna know she's not a cop. They're gonna think she knows what she's doing. She walks around the corner where somebody's trying to rob somebody or rape somebody or kill somebody they're not gonna know she's a little girl in a cop suit, they're gonna see a badge and a uniform and a gun and they're gonna blow a hole through her fuckin' head. Somebody runs up to her and asks her to help 'em, she's gonna look around and say "Where's Bill? Where's Bill?" — That's me: I'm Bill — Now, I could tell that girl likes me, it's only natural. I'm her partner, I'm a big strong father figure, whatever, gotta lot of experience, gotta lotta confidence, I'm know what I'm fuckin' doin — And that's attractive to a woman, it's attractive to anybody. So she's attracted to me. That's OK. She's human. I'm human. But maybe part of what I'm doin', part of buildin' her confidence is makin' her feel like I'm interested in her too. Maybe that makes her feel impressive. Makes her feel cocky, makes her feel like she's got something on the ball. Makes her feel like she's really a cop. Now, do I need you tellin' her I'm upstairs havin' sex with somebody on my shift so she can think I'm some kind of fuckin' maniac who's just messin' with her head, so she can lose all her confidence in me and consequently all her confidence in herself? Because of your big fuckin' flappin' fuckin' mouth? And then go out and get herself killed? Or me? Or somebody else? This is not

53

a game. We're not doormen. We're policemen. Yeah, I know, we're terrible and everything, but we're playing with our lives, and the lives of the people we're supposed to protect. So I guess I don't appreciate the fun you're havin' at my expense, and more importantly at her expense, while you're sitting around here twiddling your fuckin' thumbs and waiting for, uh, William to come around and make his rounds so you can go to sleep.

Lobby Hero
Kenneth Lonergan

Comic

Bill (thirties to forties)

Bill, a beat cop, is talking to his partner Dawn.

BILL: Damn, I swear to God — I got no reason to bullshit you: So I don't know why I'm goin' through this with you, but my friend Jim lives upstairs with Amy Heinvald, it's her apartment — And that's all there is to it. I hardly even *know* Mrs. Heinvald and anyway, she wasn't even *there* tonight. She's outta *town*. You don't want to believe me, there's nothing I can say to you.

　　If you really want to know, I had to talk to Jim about something private which doesn't concern you and which I'm not at liberty to talk about with you. He's goin' through a hard time and some really weird, really upsetting shit, and I can't talk about it because it would be a breach of privacy. You don't want to believe me there's nothing I can do.

　　Only, personally, I think that's a shame, because I really thought we really had something goin' between us. At least that's how I felt. I don't know: Maybe you didn't feel that way. So maybe it's for the best, you know? Because the way things have been goin' between us, I wouldn't know how else to stop it. It doesn't help that my wife and I are like — I don't even know what — like we don't even know each other any more. I mean I respect her, she's my wife, she's the mother of my children, I'll never say a word against her as long as I live, but it's like we're strangers. And it's been like that for three years. If it wasn't for the kids, we wouldn't be together and that's the truth. You want me to be honest? I'll be honest: This is very hard for me to say but I haven't felt like this about somebody — I don't even know when. I don't know if I ever felt this way about somebody. It's new to me.

55

And I'm scared. You know, I think I'm a little bit like you: I could face down twenty bad guys and I wouldn't blink an eye. But somethin' like this, and the whole world starts goin' around my head. Because when I'm with you, I really feel like you are the real thing, and everything else seems like bullshit to me. You want me to be honest? That's as honest as I get.

Lobby Hero

Kenneth Lonergan

Comic

Bill (thirties to forties)

Bill, a beat cop, is talking to Jeff, a front-desk guard in a luxury apartment building, about having been "betrayed" by his partner Dawn.

BILL: So you know what they did to me this afternoon, thanks to you and your girlfriend?

They bumped me off the list for my gold shield. Seven years I been waiting to get on that list, and now I gotta wait another year at least. Or maybe two. Or maybe more, before I could get back on it. And maybe never. That's a loss for the community. OK? It's a personal loss to me, but it's a primary loss for the community and I don't mind sayin' that. And all because that fuckin' bitch does not understand what it means to behave like a professional.

And you know what else she did? She made a bitter enemy of every uniform cop in the city. She is ostracized in this Department as of now. Forever. Because maybe the brass'll get on my ass for making a little mistake, but the rest of the cops don't give two shits about that. What they care about is backing people up, sticking to your man, and not selling him out to the ADA because he's cheatin' on his wife with somebody else besides you. Not that I consider this cheating. But never mind that. And OK, I got a little overzealous and sometimes put two cents in where nobody's asking for it, but is that some kind of crime? I only do it cause I care. Yeah. I know that sounds corny, but I do. I care. I cared about William and what happened, and all he had to do was tell me to mind my business, or anything like that, and I would have stayed out of it. But no. He's gotta abuse my confidence and make me look like an asshole in front of the whole goddamn division and every fuckin' muckety-muck whose ass I been kissing for the last four years. I mean I just can't believe it. I can't believe the sense of betrayal. I really can't.

The Luckiest Girl in the World
Rian Jairell

Dramatic

R.C. (thirties)

> *R.C. is a dangerous man. He is talking to his partner Hirsh, another*
> *dangerous man.*

R.C.: And he's comin' at me full bore and I'm just standin' there. I'm just
standin' and he's comin' at me. Now he's got a knife. You think that's
dangerous. Well, yeah, it is. Very fucking dangerous . . . but, it —
see, the way he held it, it was the way he held the knife that it gave
me a sense of . . . confidence. 'Cause you got guys that know knives.
They practice with them every day. Am I right? I'm one of those guys.
I know what it's like. Not one of *those* guys that just goes to a fly
store and buys a knife. No.

See and *that's* where the confidence comes in. I know by the way
he holds, he don't know how to use — just to use a knife. He's worried. He's never stabbed anything. He doesn't know how it feels to
put a blade through something that's *living*.

And . . . he's scared. We're standin' there. There we stand. And
you can tell. I mean, just by the eyes. My eyes and his eyes. You know
when you look at someone and you just *know*. You look into that
face and those eyes and you just know — knowing that confidence —
I mean, the kid is ten years younger than me. He thinks he's gonna
take me out?

I have a major dilemma here. I don't know what to do. I know
what I wanna do, but not what to do, so . . . I mean, this is a very
sticky situation. *(Referring to the donuts.)* You wanna donut? So I says
to the kid, I says, "What's a matter with you? Huh? What's a matter with you? What the fuck's a matter with you?" He's starin' me

down, *tryin'* to stare me down — with the knife, and I go, "Listen, you. I have a very serious problem with what you're trying to do. Now, you just cool your jets." Then he takes a plunge at me. Misses but — I say, "Who do you think you are? You got a problem, this ain't the way to fix it. That ain't the way things are, boy." So he comes at me. On the drop of a dime he's comin', just like that. Tryin' to freight train my ass. I move right out the way. Grab his arm, the one with the knife, and push him back and throw 'im into the wall. I take a chair. And these chairs. Not like good chairs, ya know. Flimsy. Weak. I take this chair, hit him right in the back. Goes to the ground crying.

The little bastard got up. He fucking got up. Still held the knife like a goddamn jackoff tool. And he got up. But then . . . I give him a motorcycle kick right in the knee. Down he goes, he goes down and I tell ya, he's not getting up. *(Beat.)* So I had to drag his ass to the principal's office, you just don't do that to a teacher.

The Luckiest Girl in the World

Rian Jairell

Dramatic

Hirsh (thirties)

Hirsh is talking to R.C., the same age.

HIRSH: You should just see it. Then you'd know. Know what it's like. Him sitting on the couch. Middle of the night. Listenin' to that. You could hear the moans all over the goddamn house. Just him sitting in the dark with a small tear rollin' down his face. See, I used to be confused. All these strange guys in the house. I didn't know. When I got older, boy, I laid the shit on the line. I threw some of 'em out. I mean, my dad's not gonna stick up for us, then I will. I watched her walk around the house, like she was practicin', ya know. Just like your sister. For all these men. And he just watched her. Let it go, fine, it was nothin'. The clothes she started wearin'. Like she was so high-fallutin. So goddamn special. It got to the point when I had to hit her a few times. Smack her, 'cause *he* ain't gonna. Tell her ta knock that shit off. She'd cool off for a while, then start bringin' 'em back. I don't know how many times I warned her. I mean, I fuckin' whacked her hard a few times, but to . . . uh . . . no avail. *(Pause.)* And you know what happened to him? The guy couldn't hurt anything, just as frail as — she drove him to that. She drove him to do something that he could never have done. Ever. He comes home. Hard day at work. He's pissed. Wants some sex to get out the aggression, right? She's drunker than shit. Keeps tellin' 'im how she hates him. How she wishes he would die. How small his pecker is. And he can't take it. After all those nights on the couch. This one night, he can't take it. The one night my mom has *her sister* stayin' at the house. The bastard walks in the sister's room. Tries to get fresh with her. She resisted just a little, just a tiny bit . . . and he let loose, boy. Started

60

hittin' her . . . like she was a punchin' bag. Every fist, every swing, every time, all he was thinkin', man, was those nights. All those nights. Sittin' on the couch. I mean, he almost killed her. So he gets put away for sexual assault and almost killin' someone. And the one crime he committed, the only crime, was marrying that woman. The wrong woman. All wrong. And I'll tell you this, if my wife ever did that to me — what my mom did. I'd kill her.

The Luckiest Girl in the World
Rian Jairell

Dramatic

Hirsh (thirties)

Hirsh is talking to R.C., the same age.

HIRSH: Messy. I wanted to make it real messy. The kinda messy that makes you gag . . . and I knew what I had to accomplish. Went back to the truck, found my old buck knife, still dirty from fishing. Covered with fish blood and fish guts. I snuck upstairs to Abby's bedroom. And I watched them. I watched every move they made. Then you know, when the two got done . . . *(Almost says it.)* when they finished . . . kid went to take a piss or get a sandwich, and you know she's got all that expensive meat. She's got money. Gotta have the best. Brand names. I walked in the bedroom. Turkey, roast beef . . . hickory smoked. While he was puttin' on the Provolone cheese, I was up in the room havin' a nice, sweet, last talk with her. Tell her what's what. *(Pause.)* Then I cut her throat. That real rusty blade, so she could feel how hard I was tryin' to open her up. It didn't come so easy, so she could really feel me prying away, jabbing into her. Then I cut up her other arteries and veins. Bed was full of blood. I hid, turned off the light. Kid came back. Slipped into bed. Somethin' ain't right. See, and it got real messy. And I did the same thing to him. *(Pause.)*

Madonna

Don Nigro

Comic

Nietzsche (twenties to forties)

> *In this surreal comic fantasy about artists, philosophers, and playwrights,*
> *the philosopher Nietzsche spews out his nightmare visions.*

NIETZSCHE: So you've come back to visit your friend despair, have you?
You want me to relieve your suffering, do you? Well, as I am no longer
that pathetic bag of guts people once called Nietzsche, but am trans-
figured into my true state as GOD THE FATHER ALMIGHTY,
MAKER OF SEX AND DEATH, FROM WHENCE I SHALL
COME TO MOURN THE QUICK AND THE NOT SO
QUICK — I was saying to Saint Theresa I said, dear, I've been trying to remember all of my names, as they tell me God has nine bil-
lion names, but the only ones I can recall are Hans, Fritz, and Rupert,
and of course the time in the garden when giant rabbits were nib-
bling the nipples of Cosima Wagner in the spring, oh, in the spring
it is best to be God because one can forgive everybody and sit on
the sofa and there will be no more hate or death and the mad king
gallops on a pale horse through corn stubble and the beggar drowns
in the ocean of madness where walnuts are soft and when you kiss
women you come away with a mouth full of grass, HAH, caught
you again, you thought I was going to say SHIT, but Nebuchadnezzar
ate grass and I am him also on alternate leap years as you well know
who love and worship me and are my fan club, SEE, SEE, the great
mistake we have made, the Devil and I, we forgot to wear our trousers
to the opera, but don't worry, folks, in the fourth act the Valkyries
lose weight from all the sweating, and their horns smell like goats,
who are also God, and I sing the CRUCIFIED CRUCIFIED
THRICE KISSED DIONYSUS OF ALL GOAT LOVERS THAT
IT IS ONLY NECESSARY TO HAVE INTERCOURSE ONE

TIME IN ONE'S LIFE TO CONTRACT THE MOST HORRI-
BLE DISEASES IMAGINABLE AND THEREAFTER TO ROT
AND ROT INTO GOD AND GOD and I love the little bluebirds
because they kiss me with their little sister tongues, and have we found
love yet? Have you, who watch me with bewilderment and ill-con-
cealed contempt found love? I am the Prince of Love, and woman
is the final card, we play the final card and we are lost and she is lost
but play we must and breasts are nice and stomachs but the best is
strawberry moonlight which I eat for supper every morning rain or
groan, go on, you know you can't resist her, suffering is good for you,
believe me, I'm an expert on this, I have headaches that deafen me,
hammer me, knock me out for days, stomach cramps, I vomit blood,
have fevers, chills, hideous nightmares, sweats, hallucinations, am
nearly blind, and when I write my eyeballs swell and fill with tears
from strain and I work at my desk for ten hours a day and when I
creep finally to bed at night my mind is racing and I take opiates
which make me vomit again, yes, life is very precious, go wallow in
a woman's flesh, for once your flesh is next to hers then nothing else
can matter ever and she soon is gone. If I had a woman, do you think
I would endure all this, just to write books that nobody ever reads?
What do you think, I'm crazy? So peace, my children, go on and
dance and love and hate and suffer and do not know why, you're wiser
than I, though you must die, world without end, I mend.

My Sweetheart's the Man in the Moon

Don Nigro

Comic

Harry K. Thaw (twenties)

> *This fantastic comic drama imagines the true story of the first "crime of the century," the murder of Stanford White by Harry K. Thaw, a demented young rich man who here is talking to Comstock, a crusader against vice.*

HARRY: Mr. Comstock, I have the greatest respect for the work
    you're doing at the Society for the Prevention
    of Vice, and for your heroic efforts to rid
    the American nation of fornication and masturbation.
    That's why I want to bring to your attention
    the fact that Stanford White has deflowered to date,
    by my careful calculations, a grand total of
    three hundred seventy-eight virgins. It's true, I swear
    on my mother's bronze testicles. This man has built
    the tower of Babel in Madison Square Garden,
    a place consecrated to orgies and the habitual
    debauching of underage girls by a gang of artists
    and other perverts. The ground floor's a toy store.
    The screams of girls can be heard in Portugal.
    Unspeakable cruelties are practiced there
    in a room entirely covered with funhouse mirrors.
    Thousands of girls have been lost in his vast collection
    of pornographic smuttage, much of which
    I've examined myself, for research purposes only.
    There are paintings of lewd French acrobats, I'll pay you
    to have him followed. I mean, of course, I'll make

generous donations to your society.
And I want you to know that, I, like you, act not
for my own gratification, but for the sanctity
of the American home, for the purity of
the little American wife. For the unstained bloomers
of millions of Pittsburgh virgins. I myself
am only the humble instrument of Providence.
So who should I make the check out to?
And Comstock looks at me with his beady little
Puritan eyes, and he says, oh, you can just
make it out to me personally if you like.
That's how I can tell he's a good American. Good
Americans always want the check made out
in their own name. Although I myself would have asked
for unmarked twenty dollar bills just in case
those people from Venus are watching. But that diabolical
bastard White hired his own private detectives
to follow the private detectives I hired to follow
him. So I figure Comstock's detectives can follow
White's detectives while White's are following mine.
I want to know every move he makes. This man
takes a dump, I want to know how long the turd was.
And I want room service. And don't send me any
more of those goddamned prunes. Do you hear me? Take down
your pants, you little piece of crap. Do you think
I don't know what's going on here, sister? I know
what's going on. I can read the wrinkles in
the folds of your sweet petootie. Come here, honey bunch.
I know how to be good to a woman. Not like
that goat-lover Stanford White. Look in his brain,
and there's nothing but broken clocks and shattered mirrors
in there, yet all of them seem to want to rut
with him. The beautiful, the innocent,
the young. While I, the man who loves, the man
who knows what love is, am left standing in

the rain, my straw hat bent, dogs pissing
on my leg. It isn't right. I do not weep
for myself. I weep for the poor deflowered maidens,
stained forever by the toxic semen
of that rutting hyena. Such animals make one suspect
God's mental state. But if the Lord won't help me,
I know where I can obtain a very handsome
little gun.

Onionheads
Jesse Miller

Dramatic

Jeb (twenties)

> *Jeb, a poor, young dirt farmer, has picked up an onion and is talking
> to it.*

JEB: *(To onion.)* You ol' dried up, sour, enemy of the eyes! T'ain't got
enough juice fer a thirsty man to squeeze outta ya on the side of the
road. Hun'erd an' one awful blisterin' heat bangin' down on my head
ever' day, an' still I carry you on my back like yer gonna squirt some
kinda oil on my joints an' quench me . . . save me, er somepin. Might
as well git blood from a turnip, crops from them black fiel's, or hope
from a road 'at's seen more death than a war. Foolish talk. An' what's
worse, is I got you fer my good luck charm. Somepin wrong there.
Somepin wrong. *(Beat.)* But if you think I's gonna shrivel up an' die
like the rest of yer selfish, skinny little friends, you got another thing
comin'! Yessir, 'cause, I'll wrap my han's aroun' anythin' to git my
lan' back. Grapes, peaches, lettuce, it's all the same to me. Know what
else? They's got manners. They ain't nothin' like the likes of y'all. They
don't feel the need to leave their smell on ya fer markin', markin' like
you owns the han's 'at killed ya. Manners. Somepin y'all better learn
if ya wanna live in this world of con-see-quence an' mishap. Oh, but
you don't wanna live, do ya? Y'all is about dyin', dyin' 'fore you say
a word to the fella 'at spent more time tendin' to you than his own
children. 'At's sweet. As sweet as you git. *(Beat.)* I'm talkin' to an
onion. *(Lookin' to heaven.)* Damn you Mama, fer not pumpin' me
fulla sense. Instead, ya gimme some a that silly 'at Aloysius speaks
from every pitiful pore. People gonna talk. They's gonna say, "Who
was 'at Jeb Tidwell? 'At crazy . . . . good lookin' . . . well-built boy
we found dead on Highway Sixty-Six, not a drop a juice in 'im? . . .
Jus' an onion by his side, laughin'." Laughin' like an onion will . . .

Platonically Incorrect

Darlene Hunt

Comic

Steve (twenties to thirties)

> *It's Steve's first day in therapy. He is talking to a therapist whom we never see. He is out of breath and anxious.*

STEVE: Hi. I apologize. I'm late. I'm bad. I wrote your address in my palm pilot and then I left it at home — oh, I put you under chiropractor instead of therapist just in case somebody might see — anyway, I do have this knot in my back — no, just kidding. So I left my palm pilot at home, smart, I know. Did you know you're not listed? . . . Good thing this is only therapy and not a first date, right? . . . which is actually why I'm here . . . I have problems with relationships. Specifically staying in them. That's probably pretty common, huh? . . . Yes? No? Hello, is this thing on? . . . Ok, so. Where were we? Me. Crazy. Relationships. Right. D said I should tell you . . . oh, D, that's Darlene, my best friend. Write that down. You'll hear a lot about her. Not too much, though, it's my hour, remember? . . . OK, not much of a laugher, are you? Anyway, D says I use my sense of humor to get women's attention but then I get bored in relationships because while I'm walking on barrels to make them laugh, nobody ever makes me laugh. *(Beat.)* Whoa. I think Oprah calls that a lightbulb moment . . . Oh, and listen. When you start tweaking my personality, I have a very feminine music collection I wonder if you could do anything about. You know, see if we can't butch it up a little bit.

Praying for Rain
Robert Lewis Vaughan

Dramatic

Marc (late teens)

> *Marc is an ex-high-school jock having to face an identity crisis now that he can no longer do sports due to an injury.*

MARC: I loved playing sports. God I . . . I was great at football and base-ball and I really loved that. I didn't care too much about anything else. My grades were always okay and like, I passed, and didn't have to worry about getting kicked off the teams, so . . . God I . . . And there was this girl, Erin . . . ? She did track. And. Well, I mean, I was . . . I wasn't like one of the rich kids, and didn't . . . Erin wasn't either but she was really popular, and we kind of hung around with different people, but she was always nice though . . . I kind of liked her. A lot. I mean I . . . It was like . . . what was my history?

I didn't think about that? You know? I was . . . I was gonna be eighteen soon and . . . I'm just some kid, you know? I'm just some dumb kid that thought everything was kind of okay. You know? I was really good at what I loved doing when I was a sophomore and then when I was a junior . . . And nobody in my family ever even like thought about college, you know? They never mentioned any-thing like that — it was like — when are you gonna get a job. But at school they were talking to me about college. My stupid brother dropped out of school and just works where he can . . . I mean. I don't know what he ever cared about. But they were talking to me about . . . How do you know what people care about? How do you know what you care about?

Reality
Curtiss I' Cook

Dramatic

Jimmy (twenties)

Jimmy is a young black man testifying to Rev. Sweets.

JIMMY: It's for them . . . Charlie, Chucky, boy . . . they watch and say nothing, they laugh and make comments on our lives as if they have a right to. Clean up our neighborhoods. From who? From our young brothers, that's the easy way to go. We can see what they do as they sit and watch us as if they have nothing wrong in their lives . . . but they do . . . they have many things wrong. But this gives them a chance to escape that, to get away from that bill that needs to be paid, that person who needs to be talked to . . . We can't get away from our problems because I'm here with this . . . *(Indicates the gun.)* . . . and we are going to talk them out, because they will help us. They will help me. I didn't kill that child! She did it! She didn't mean it . . . I didn't kill Sabrina. He did, with his ignorance, and he blames me for letting her die . . . for letting her bleed and die . . . Get them off that corner, whose corner, it's their corner, why should we get them off of it!! Who's inside the building that's on the corner and what are they doing? Are they helping us or themselves . . . they watch, I see you looking at me . . . Stop looking at me unless you have something to say to me . . . unless you want to add to what I'm saying . . . Stop looking at me or I'll shoot you! I'll shoot everyone! I DIDN'T KILL THAT BABY!! SHE DIDN'T MEAN TO . . .

The Resurrectionist
Kate Chell

Dramatic

Pond (forties to fifties)

Pond is a detective in seventeenth-century England.

POND: Don't be such a wide-eyed innocent. If death is inevitable, and incidentally, it is; I say if that is the case, then to waste the opportunity afforded us by the passing of a fellow human is a crime equal to murder itself. If we don't take that opportunity, we have only ourselves to blame for our ignorance and only our ignorance to blame for our inability to delay, even to circumvent, the inevitable. We know intelligent men ourselves who still prescribe leeches to thin the blood. Men who drone on about the humors, carry herbs to ward off foul air, still expect the king's touch to cure scrofula — men who look at the Bill of Mortality every week when it's printed and wonder why deaths stay so high. Look at the goddamn barber-surgeons, for Christ's sake! But take a man like William Harvey, an anatomist with the gall to dissect his own kin and look at what he's discovered. Blood courses through the body, it circulates; and look what he dares to study now, the very development of life in the fetus! How can we not dare that boldness, Jeffrey? *(He goes and shuts the door.)* Death can be made to serve us. It's what you did two nights ago and what you'll do every time you pay out a sum from your pocket to possess the left-behind wastes of mortality, Jeffrey. And rightly so, I say. Don' look indignant. You're an anatomist now. You'll learn to make it serve you.

Romance
Barbara Lhota

Comic

Mick (twenties to thirties)

Mick is in a church after a funeral, drunkenly talking to God.

MICK: You know what I've been thinkin', God. The reason our whole world has gone to crap and the idiot politicians keep gettin' reelected and the ozone layer turned into a greenhouse thing, and the Red Sox keep losin' is that there are a lot words with no meanin' out there. You follow? Words people use to create misunderstandings, to confuse instead of to uh, uh, uh, *(Several arm gestures.)* communicate. *(Pause.)* You want examples? That's fair. But remember this is a, a, an embryonic idea. Naaaah, it's a new idea. Forget the embryo, it has too much to do with women. And that's a whole other mess. Okay, so examples. There's plenty. I just have to think. *(He leans against the pew and pounds his head with his fist.)* Pre-boarding. A perfect example. What does it mean? Stewards call passengers on planes to preboard. Logic says, there is only boarding and not boarding. Now this word has the prefix *pre,* meaning before. So pre-boarding would be BEFORE boarding. Only that's not what it means. Because the preboarders actually board the plane during pre-boarding. Now, these pre-boarders are really special people. They're people with first-class seats. Rich people. Somehow people with first-call seats don't have to truly board. They magically float onto the plane during PRE-BOARDING! Get it?! But the word doesn't mean what you'd think it would. Does it?! It confuses! It should be called "early boarding" or "first-class boarding," or "Take up all the storage space boarding"! *(Pause. Looks down at the bottle.)*

I was gonna be pre-boarding tomorrow for the first time. For the first time, I was gonna be a SPECIAL person, a first-class passenger who could PRE-BOARD. I could still do it, but it wouldn't have the same meaning. Would it? *(He sits, puts head in hands.)* Shit!

Romance
Barbara Lhota

Comic

Mick (twenties to thirties)

Mick is talking to Miriam, who he has just met in a church after a funeral.

MICK: The family was spread over the pews. He isn't Catholic exactly, but close enough. The brothers and sisters, all married, sat right here. And there . . . *(He points.)* there sat Mom, hair done up high. So they do the whole walk down the isle, everything's smooth. Everybody's pretty. Until they get to the part where ya got to, where ya gotta, *(Slaps his hand.)* Wham! You know, tell it like it is. And he gets to askin' her if she wants to spend the rest of life with him and there's this pause. And he thinks — "Wow, she's makin' this dramatic!" But the pause goes on. He looks over at her and she doesn't move. She stands there. Still. Only he can hear her breathing. He tries to catch her eye to see if she's just nervous, but she ignores him. He looks over at Mom and her forehead's all wrinkled, tense and her hair starts unraveling. And then, this knot forms in his throat — like a lump, but kinda twisted, and it gets real dry. And he thinks, he can say something, do something, tell a joke, he can stop this. But the only thing that comes out of his mouth was a little moan. A little cry — a noise, so small. You can barely understand that he's sayin' "Marie, Marie." She turns to him with a face so full up of sorry. His sisters, his brother keep tellin' him that it was cold feet — cold feet. But in that instant, he knew she didn't love him. She wanted, wished, hoped to, but she just didn't. She wanted to, but she didn't. Didn't love him. And the whole thing turned into a Goddamn funeral. *(Pause)* So don't tell me about lonely.

Scent of the Roses
Lisette Lecat Ross

Dramatic

Van George (forties)

This play takes place in South Africa. Van George is an art dealer.

VAN GEORGE: Talk to you about painting . . . ? Well, I suppose, in simple terms — no insult intended. For me, painting . . . it's not just
technique, it's . . . With painting you have to see differently. You have
to . . . to *listen* with your eyes. Look around you, Miss Wynand. See
the tricks the light plays on our world, the transformations it creates! With light! Look! No, *look* at it! The most ordinary — *(He looks
around.)* The basket. These roses. All illusion. Color — what is it?
It's light! And, you work backwards, you see, and brush stroke by
brush stroke you build the color. You create the light! You capture
illusion with another illusion! Look at perspective! More illusion! But
Art is more. Much more, it's . . . Wherever we look, we look for meaning. It's what we do, all of us. We have to do that, it's how we're built.
And when you think of it! *(Gazes round the garden.)* All this . . . !
The Sleeping Beauty . . . The sky . . . The whole thing! Who could
not paint? *(Suddenly feeling exposed.)* Anyway. You've come to the
wrong man, Miss Wynand, I wouldn't know how to begin to tell you.
(Almost pedagogically.) Of course you can't paint anything — not
well — without technique.

Seeking the Genesis
Kia Corthron

Dramatic

Justin (sixteen)

Justin is a violent gang member.

JUSTIN: King's, Christmas help. I fill out my application, then they set me at this table, alone. In the quiet I hear it: big clock on the wall tick tick. My stomach warm, tight. This is a *test!* 1: Sale cassettes are three for a dollar. Customer buys one. How much change he get? Easy 66 and two-thirds. I go to 2. Wait a minute. Back to 1. Erase the two-thirds. Erase 66, round to 67, 67 cents change. Go to 2. Hold it. Don't they round against the customer? Store's advantage? So 66 change. I think. 66 cents change, I erase 67, make it 66. Erase 67. Erase — hole in the paper. I get back to 1 later, 2: Toy cars are 45 cent apiece. Customer hands you two sixty. How many cars she bought? Point four five into two sixty, simple. Five and seven-ninths, dammit! Five cars or six? Almost six. Do they mean she gets change? They must mean change. They don't say nothin' 'bout change, *hey!* Is this a trick question? They say *toy* cars are 45 cent, but then ask how many *cars* she buy. They mean *real* cars now? If they do I say answer is zero. Time runnin' out, gotta write somethin'. Five and seven-ninths. 3: 25-dollar shoes are 25 percent off. How much they cost? Point 75 times 25 dollars: eighteen seventy-five. "Time!" Man comes back, takes my test. He says I'm the only person ever get right problem 3, the percent, hard one, and wrong the two easies.

Splash Hatch on the E Going Down

Kia Corthron

Dramatic

Erry (eighteen)

Erry is talking to Thyme, even younger, the mother of his child.

ERRY: *(Pause.)* The big black ball swing back. I watch it, eager, envious like always: someday I be promoted to wreckin' ball operator. I go in, my regular job, so far this dream's quite true to life, siff through the havoc the demolishment, half the buildin' demolitioned to ashes. Dust so thick I see nothin', walk miles and miles through fourth floor blindin' dust. Finally it's clearin'. There you are, this blow-up baby pool, you in a bikini with a nine-month belly. "Here, Erry." You toss me the beach ball. I toss it back but ain't you that catches it, now the pool occupied by my three-year-old son. Next, I hear him laughin', somewhere. I follow the sound, find him. Sof' chair by a fireplace, this ritzy place this woodsy cottage is ours, we live here. Readin' a baby book he laughs out loud the funny story. I approach. "Read it, Daddy." The pictures is red and yella and purple, the words big as onions. I can't read it. I stare, I stare, I look it over, this sure is a baby book but it make no sense to me. My son's eyes turned up to his daddy, waitin'. I recognize *G*. I recognize *L. T.* I make this laugh. He start laughin' again. "See?" he say. I laugh hard, hard, I roll on the floor, my belly hurt. Eventu'ly, out the corner a my eye I notice my boy long been done with his laughter but I don't dare stop.

2½ Jews
Alan Brandt

Dramatic

Marc (early thirties)

> *Marc is a corporate lawyer who has just been named a partner in his firm. He responds to his father, a famous civil rights lawyer who sub-consciously competes with his son and who, unlike Marc, has placed his career ahead of his family.*

MARC: Nothing is safe from that bitter anger of yours. Nothing! It twists everything . . . your son gets made a partner in a top law firm and all you see is a greedy yuppie scurrying for bucks instead of choos-ing to work for his father. How could this shallow materialist be the son of Nathan Minter, the Albert Schweitzer of the legal profession . . . Saint Nathan, protector of the oppressed? My God! Doesn't the boy realize that by not joining daddy's firm he missed the chance of being referred to in the *Post* and *Time* magazine as the apostle Marc . . . son of the "magician," heir to the savior? Or does that last allu-sion make me anti-Semitic like my mother, who has the gall to enjoy someone who has time for her . . . who speaks TO her not AT her? You can't even enjoy your . . . "Great" . . . daughter's happiness with her kids and her husband. I can't even run two miles faster than you at half your age, without you whining like a wounded animal. I can't run a fucking marathon, unless I and the whole world knows that without you, I couldn't do it. Injured hamstring? Bullshit! You're not running it this year because I am and you're scared shitless that I'll finish and you won't. Why can't I run faster than you and maybe longer than you? Why can't your wife want something that, for what-ever reason, you haven't been able to give her? Well, goddamn it, they can and I can. If I can run twenty-six miles, three hundred eighty-five yards, I'll do it damn it. And if I can do it in less than your four hours and nineteen minutes I'll do that too. I am not your goddam baby boy.

Wrong Mountain
David Hirson

Seriocomic

Cliff (twenties to thirties)

> *Cliff, a young playwright at a playwriting festival, is talking to Dennett, a cynical poet in his forties to fifties who doesn't think much of the theater.*

CLIFF: *(Diffidently, but with a growing sense of self-possession.)* But Wilde was a *playwright*, wasn't he? . . . as *well* as a poet. What makes you believe that he would have discriminated between a middle-class theater audience and the audience for *poetry*, which could be described in equally pejorative terms as a bunch of pimply undergraduates and the circle of bitter, unread poets and critics they hope someday to become. *(Diffidently self-possessed.)* I mean . . . if you're going to have contempt for one audience, you might as well have contempt for them all. It's not as if readers of poetry are an especially incorruptible breed, nor that poets are any less likely than playwrights to be sycophants. Dishonest artists can be found in any field, often at the very top. Hell, if you don't think most so-called "serious" poetry isn't *corn-ball* . . . *(Waving Dennett's book of poems in the air.)* . . . you can't be reading very much "serious" poetry. *(He laughs.)* Sorry if this sounds rude, but I find it hard to imagine anything more cornball than believing that one art form is more or less cornball than another. And all of your anxiety about the middle class — what the middle class thinks, and what the middle class wants, and what the middle class approves of — sounds to me suspiciously . . . well . . . *middle-class.* Or at least governed by a suspiciously middle-class idea of success. And if that's what you want, then . . . yes! . . . everything you say is true . . . you'd better do your best to figure out what will please the crowd and . . . give it to them. But unless you make the demeaning assumption that an audience's taste can, or should, be ascertained by the application of some cynical calculus, nothing prevents you from expressing yourself truthfully and hoping that it's appreciated . . . and if it *is,* great! . . . and if it *isn't,* well, too bad . . . but whether it's appreciated or not can't be the *point!* It can't be the measure of success . . . !

PLATONICALLY INCORRECT by Darlene Hunt. © 2001, 2002 by Darlene Hunt. Reprinted by permission of the author. Contact: Abrams Artists Agency, Attn: Charmaine Ferenczi, 275 Seventh Avenue, 26th Floor, New York, NY 10001.

PRAYING FOR RAIN by Robert Lewis Vaughan. © 2001 by Robert Lewis Vaughan. Reprinted by permission of the author. Contact: Writers and Artists Agency, 19 W. 44th Street, Suite 1000, New York, NY 10036. Published by Dramatists Play Service.

REALITY by Curtiss I' Cook. © by Curtiss I' Cook. Reprinted by permission of Acme Talent & Literary Agency, Attn: Leo Bookman, 875 Avenue of the Americas, #2108, New York, NY 10001. Published in *Plays and Playwrights 2002.*

THE RESURRECTIONIST by Kate Chell. © 2001 by Kate Chell. Reprinted by permission of the author. Contact: Axial Entertainment, 20 West 21st Street, 8th Floor, New York, NY 10010. Published in *Plays and Playwrights 2002.*

ROMANCE by Barbara Lhota. © 2001 by Barbara Lhota. Reprinted by permission of the author. Contact: Smith and Kraus, Inc., P.O. Box 127, Lyme, NH 03768. Fax: (603) 643-1831. Published by Smith and Kraus, Inc. in *Women Playwrights: The Best Plays of 2001.*

SCENT OF THE ROSES by Lisette Lecat Ross. © 2001 by Lisette Lecat Ross. Reprinted by permission of the author. Contact: Samuel Liff, c/o William Morris Agency, 1325 Avenue of the Americas, New York, NY 10019. Published by Dramatists Play Service.

SEEKING THE GENESIS by Kia Corthron. © 2002 by Kia Corthron. Reprinted by permission of Sarah Jane Leigh. For North American stage performance rights (excluding first-class professional performance), contact: Dramatists Play Service, Inc. For all other rights, contact: Sarah Jane Leigh, c/o ICM, 40 West 57th Street, New York, NY 10019. Published by Dramatists Play Service.